Charlie's Gift

~~~

A Story of Love and Loss, Doubt and Faith

By

Pauline Dotzler Flynn

With

Drawings by Sharon Hickey

Dear Ham,

May your mother always be a presence in your mother

Pauline

Charlie's Gift

A Story of Love and Loss, Doubt and Faith

By

Pauline Dotzler Flynn

With

Drawings by Sharon Hickey

Countinghouse Press, Inc.
Bloomfield Hills, Michigan

Charlie's Gift

A Story of Love and Loss, Doubt and Faith

By Pauline Dotzler Flynn

ISBN 978-0-9786191-5-2
ISBN 0-9786191-3-7

Published by Countinghouse Press, Inc. Address all inquiries to: Countinghouse Press, Inc., 6632 Telegraph Road, #311, Bloomfield Hills, MI 48301. Phone 248.642.7191. Email: nuhuguenot@aol.com; Web: www.countinghousepress.com

Publisher's Cataloging-In-Publication Data: Charlie's gift: a story of love and loss, doubt and faith / by Pauline Dotzler Flynn.
P: 140. ill.; cm.
ISBN 978-0-9786191-5-2
ISBN 0-9786191-3-7
1. Flynn, Pauline Dotzler. 2. Flynn, Charles Francis, 1940-1988. 3. Widowhood. 4. Bereavement—Psychological aspects. 5. Bereavement—Religious aspects. 6. Bereavement—Poetry. I. Title.
CIP # BF575.G7 F559 2009
155.6443

Printed in the United States of America by Color House Graphics, Grand Rapids, Michigan. Cover design by Sans Serif, Inc., Saline, MI. This is a book of inspirational writing. It does not claim to be, is not, and does not constitute political, medical, nutritional, or legal advice. The opinions in this book are solely the opinions of the author.

Dedication

For my daughters Liz, Katie and Laura, each of whom embodies, in her own unique way, the best aspects of Charlie's soul—his playfulness, his love of the natural world, and his determination and persistence in making this world a better place for all.

Contents

Acknowledgments

Many people support me emotionally and embrace me with their love. Surrounded by this loving support I was able to navigate the challenging waters of Charlie's illness and death and to make the transition to a joyful life as a single woman. I want to thank all who helped me along the way.

My friends Cora Eng, Claudia Scott, Mary Jo Wilson, Binx Mahoney, Mary Gold, and many, many other friends who cried with me, listened to me with patience, held my hand or placed an arm on my shoulder when I needed warmth, and who judiciously offered their own insight and wisdom. My colleagues Jean Sweeney, Susan McCarthy, Mari Suarez, Carol Poplin, and Fr. Tuck Grinnell who prayed for me and with me and always made time to listen to me.

My sister Kathy Garry, my brothers, Jim Dotzler, Robert Dotzler, Jack Dotzler and Frank Dotzler, their spouses, my nieces and nephews, and my aunts and cousins who have always held me in their loving embrace and whom I always knew I could count on in difficult moments. Charlie's sister Marian Flynn, her husband Bill Berlin, my niece Kathryn Flynn and all of Charlie's relatives who have embraced me even more completely after Charlie's death. They make it possible to know that the word family means love.

Molly Jones who helped me to face the challenges that would bring me peace—writing this book and recognizing that its theme revolved around the issue of faith and doubt. Georgia Robertson who helped me to discover ways to embrace the poetry muse. Sherry Hickey who provided the delightful drawings and meticulously proofread the manuscript. Len Charla who offered important suggestions for the manuscript that gave it greater depth and wholeness and who found it worthy of publishing. To these people and many, many others who make my life whole. Thank you all. This book would not have been possible without your presence in my life.

-Arlington, Virginia
April 2, 2011

Sonnet 43

How do I love thee? Let me count the ways.
I love thee to the depth and breadth and height
My soul can reach, when feeling out of sight
For the ends of Being and ideal Grace.
I love thee to the level of every day's
Most quiet need, by sun and candlelight.
I love thee freely, as men strive for Right;
I love thee purely as they turn from Praise.
I love with the passion put to use
In my old griefs, and with my childhood's faith.
I love thee with a love I seemed to lose
With my lost saints, —I love thee with the breath,
Smiles, tears, of all my life! —and if God choose,
I shall but love thee better after death.

--Elizabeth Barrett Browning

Acceptance

You are a jewel
Buried deep
Inside me
Promises kept
No dream

When he opened the door Rick found his office filled chest-high with colorful balloons. He'd been away on vacation and this was his first day back. As he had turned the doorknob about to enter the room, he had wondered about the straight pin that was conspicuously taped to the door. Letting out a good laugh, now he knew why the pin was there. He'd need it to burst all the balloons in order to make a path to his desk so that he could get back to work! He could see that his coworkers had been busy while he was gone, busy making this practical joke possible. And who was responsible? He knew right away it was Charlie Flynn. This wasn't the first time Charlie had enlisted the whole office in some lighthearted scheme as a way to help his fellow attorneys relax, have a little fun, and take themselves a bit less seriously.

Now Charlie lay in a hospital bed in our bedroom. The life force was seeping out of the once vibrant, fun-loving soul I knew and loved, my husband of 30 years. He was barely able to eat, unable to speak, and in great pain when he moved. His life hung by the thinnest of threads when I asked him a question that would change the way I came to view our relationship. This question, which tumbled off my tongue without any conscious forethought, would have profound consequences. It would open up a path to a whole new understanding of the relationship between life and death.

About a week before he died, while standing at the head of the bed, my hand resting on Charlie's bony shoulder, I asked, "Will you tell me when the angels come for you?" Charlie's strength waned visibly with each passing day, so his very definitive response surprised me. A dark, determined frown flashed across his face and his eyes glared at me, as he mouthed the word "NO!" Because he had had a laryngectomy he made no sound. But his response, which came without a moment's hesitation, was loud and clear. It resounded through my body. I knew immediately that, in the little time we had left together, I could not change his mind. I accepted his word as final.

I took a deep breath, swallowed my disappointment and resigned myself to accepting his wishes. I wanted to be at Charlie's side at the most difficult moment in our lives together, yet I didn't protest. It was his death that we were staring in the face and I knew that he would do it his way. The challenge for me would be to love him and care for him in ways that didn't interfere with his determination to die in the way he chose to. I told no one about the question I had asked Charlie. And I told no one of his disappointing response. But the memory of that moment remained hidden in my heart.

After 30 years of marriage I knew the strength of Charlie's determination and his willpower. When he had a strong opinion he never let circumstances change his mind or alter his course. His integrity, which I observed and admired from the very first night we met, had attracted me to him. Lying on our backs on the cool grass under a dark and starry sky, our bodies so close that I could feel our hearts beating in unison, I knew that this tall, lanky fellow I had just met was a strong and good man. Certainly there would be times during our marriage when his inflexible stand on some principle made me angry because I didn't agree with him, but I always admired and respected his strength of character.

While the force of Charlie's response to my question startled me, the fact that he simply answered "NO" didn't surprise me at all. He was a quiet, private, and practical man who took his faith seriously in his own very quiet, private, and practical way. Time had not changed this aspect of his personality. His faith was a faith of action and he acted on his faith in tangible ways.

To Charlie, being a man of faith meant being honest, thoughtful of others, and putting his family first. He professed his faith quietly by dedicating his life to working in a job that had a meaningful impact upon society and sharing his wealth with the poor. He was unattached to worldly things. When I first met him when he was a law student his signature casual clothing was raggedy sneakers which would later be replaced by sneakers with Velcro closings. Even as a professional attorney, he didn't believe that "clothes make the man." He owned six suits for each season, rotating them in the closet in an orderly way so that he didn't wear the same suit on the same day of the week.

While I was interested in speculating about philosophical issues and spiritual subjects, Charlie concentrated his efforts in the practical arenas of everyday life. Being respectful of others by being on time for appointments and honoring his commitment to tithe in order to make a better world were important to him. He could often be found on a Sunday morning in a soup kitchen, behind the scenes, supervising our daughters' Sunday school classmates chopping vegetables for salad so that others might eat. He not only financially supported SOME, where the hungry homeless men and women of Washington, DC can get a good balanced meal, he put himself on the front lines. Yet, he didn't talk about these commitments; he merely acted upon them. In fact, he once made a large contribution to his alma mater by sending a cashier's check so his identity wouldn't be known. I argued with him about the wisdom of sending an anonymous donation and often the opposite ways we had of approaching life led to conflict. But now, during these final moments of our lives together I didn't want to risk creating discord. I wanted to love him in ways that honored his way of being.

4

Charlie rarely got involved in theological discussions or professed his faith in words. While he wasn't worldly he was immersed in the here and now. And he was certainly much too pragmatic to concern himself with the existence of angels.

Both Charlie and I knew the New Testament stories about the angel who speaks to Mary announcing Jesus' birth, the angel who warns Joseph to take Jesus and Mary by a different route to flee from Herod's wrath, and the angels who surprise Mary Magdalene at Jesus' empty tomb and tell her that Jesus had risen. While visiting Salt Lake City during a cross-country trip, we learned about the relatively modern angel, Moroni, who shows Joseph Smith where the golden tablets of the Book of Mormon can be found. But neither Charlie nor I had ever had an experience of angels nor had we heard friends tell us of having had such an experience. I was curious about angels and had read books about how ordinary people had experienced the presence of angels in moments of crisis and about angels who are present with deceased loved ones at the moment of death.

Thinking back to the moment when the words of the question spontaneously formed on my lips, I realize that asking Charlie to tell me when the angels came for him helped to mask the pain that contemplating the impending rupture of our relationship created. The question protected him and me from facing the harshness of the reality of the permanent separation from each other. Surely, I wanted to be with him at the very last moment of our lives together, but posing the question was a way to avoid staring directly into death's ugly face and the separation of our souls that death would bring.

When I asked Charlie to tell me when the angels came for him, I wasn't certain what I believed about angels. I wasn't sure they existed and if they did exist I wasn't certain that they were involved in people's lives in our world today. When I asked Charlie to tell me when the angels came for him, I understood his lack of concern about angels, but given the circumstances of his life and the very closeness of his death, I thought that he might be more open to the existence of such heavenly beings. When I uttered the question I suspended my own uncertainty about angels and opened myself to the possibility of believing that angels do exist and are involved in the lives of ordinary people. At this tenuous moment in our lives together, I had found the courage to risk believing.

Overriding my doubt and taking the risk to make this request of Charlie would have profound consequences, as the experiences after his death would show me. However, it would be years before I fully understood the consequences of asking that question. During that time I would struggle with faith and doubt. In time I would come to more fully embrace faith, but at the same time learn the importance of doubt.

2

Destiny

Play spirit play
Let the winds
Blow freely

My once vigorous husband, who now lay helpless in bed—his bones visible from not being able to eat, his courtroom lawyer's vibrant voice quieted by a laryngectomy, was known for his quick wit and fun-loving antics.

The first time I laid eyes on Charlie he was sitting in the basket of a shopping cart outside of a bar at closing time. He had crammed his tall lanky frame into the cart at 1 AM in order to attract the attention of four young women. I was one of those women. Three girlfriends and I had driven from our homes on Long Island to the Nation's Capital for the weekend. After we had settled into our lodging late in the evening, looking for something to eat after a long drive, the four of us found what we were looking for in an establishment that advertised itself in big bold letters as "RESTAURANT." Once inside we discovered it was a bar.

My friends and I took frequent weekend trips together and, in order to facilitate decision-making on our weekend adventures, we had decided that, if we had any doubt or disagreement about what to do, we would follow the driver's choice. If we couldn't decide which restaurant to go to or whether to skip one attraction in order to spend more time at another, we looked to the driver, whose choice we followed. Since we took turns driving, this was an equitable way to handle all the little decisions that our group needed to make our trips go smoothly.

Anne, who was driving her car on this weekend adventure to Washington, elbowed me across the front seat and said, "Ask them if they want a ride." I was a quiet and shy young woman, not inclined to speak out to strange men, but since we had this "rule" about driver's choice, I felt compelled to do what she wanted. So I rolled down the window and called out in a weak voice, "Do you want a ride?" With a curious grin on his face the fellow in the shopping cart said, "Yes," and he and his friend, who had been pushing the cart, hopped into the back seat of the car. We hadn't gone a block and Anne had barely gotten her Peugeot into second gear, when the tall, lanky fellow announced, "You can let us out here." Then the two of them invited us to join them in this second bar that didn't close till an hour later. Surprised and intrigued by the playfulness of these two fellows, we accepted.

By the time the sun came up that morning an electric chemistry had been set off between Charlie and me that would only be intensified after the events of the following night. Assuring that he could find dates for all of my girlfriends, Charlie invited us to canoe to a Watergate concert. In those days, on summer evenings the National Symphony performed regularly on the banks of the Potomac at a bend in the river where stadium seating created a perfect location for a concert. (A hotel would later be built nearby which gave its name to a famous presidential scandal.) After renting four canoes at Jack's Canoes near Key Bridge, each couple set off in a canoe and began paddling downstream toward the Watergate.

I had never paddled a canoe before and I didn't know how to swim. I was a city girl, born and raised in New York City, and although I had always lived near the ocean beaches, I had never learned to swim. Naïve about canoe safety, I thought it was fun to use the paddle to splash a couple in another boat. Suddenly, the canoe that Charlie and I were in capsized, and I found myself in blackness under the canoe. But before I even understood the gravity of what had happened, Charlie had dived under the canoe and rescued me. Charlie lost his glasses and I lost a shoe in the mishap, but drenched in what was then very polluted Potomac River water, we managed to right the canoe and climb safely back in.

9

Life for Charlie and me was never the same after that evening in the murky waters of the Potomac. We had both been drawn out of our own individual worlds into a new world in which our fates were intertwined. He had saved my life and I would be forever appreciative of his quick thinking and his life-saving skill. Fortunately, he had unknowingly been preparing for this event for some time. He always claimed that as a college freshman he had been literally dragged out of his dorm room bed one Saturday morning by the swimming coach who was looking for recruits for the team. He reluctantly joined the team and would go on to become a valued team member. During the summers he would use his swimming prowess working as a lifeguard at Lake Cochituate near his home in Massachusetts.

In spite of the electricity that sparked between Charlie and me, our courtship did not go smoothly. There were several years of ups and downs in our relationship, but, finally, in December of 1967, I expected that Charlie would ask me to marry him. When he asked to borrow my car for a day, I was certain that he needed it to go to a jeweler to buy me a diamond for Christmas. Was I surprised when I opened the box and found that it contained a time bomb—a toy designed to be tossed from kid to kid like a hot potato and which after a time exploded with a loud noise! I was annoyed and disappointed with his silly antic since I was hopeful that we would get engaged, but I had to laugh at Charlie's clever playfulness. This was Charlie's way of telling me he just wasn't ready to tie the knot. Yet with his Christmas gift he revealed quite dramatically the kind of fellow he was and wasn't. He was not a romantic. He never did anything he wasn't ready to do. But he was a person who had a quick and clever mind that he loved using in playful, dramatic, and meaningful ways. He wasn't a gift giver in the conventional sense of the word, that is, buying gifts to make someone feel special, but I was to learn during our many years together that he gave many gifts to me and to my family.

Most importantly, Charlie's gag Christmas gift revealed to me that he did things in his own time. While the exploding toy was symbolic of the electric chemistry that pulsed between us, I would have to wait until Charlie was ready to get married. I would have to be patient. On Valentine's Day of the following year, we did decide to get engaged, but without a diamond ring. Together we decided against a diamond but instead to buy ourselves matching wedding bands. We chose a design that I later discovered was a love knot, a design in which two strands are intertwined with no beginning and no end.

With Charlie's dislike of shopping and lack of interest in gift giving I took over those roles for our family. The only time I could persuade him to shop with me was when we went to a toy store. Then he would enjoy shopping and make an excursion of it. With great persistence he would wander through the aisles of huge toy stores in order to discover a new game for each holiday season. In later years when our daughters were in college, he reveled in going to the toy store to get them 21 toys for their 21st birthdays. He loved the idea of packaging up all these toys, from Chinese jump ropes and bubbles to decks of playing cards and silly stickers, in the hope of surprising them with reminders of their childhood. It was his way of saying to them, "Study hard, but don't take life too seriously. Remember to take time for fun."

Not being a shopper at heart, I tired of the role. I tried harder and harder to get Charlie to join me, to no avail. So, in order to avoid the resentment that was building up in me, Charlie and I came up with an idea for a gift-free Christmas. We decided to rent cabins at Blackwater Falls State Park in the mountains of West

11

Virginia, where we would spend a week together with our daughters and with those members of Charlie's family and my family who could join us. This week in the mountains would be our gift to our loved ones. The first "rule" we declared was that the only gifts we would exchange would be $10 grab bag gifts that had to be funny. The other "rule" was: Each person would bring an idea for an activity that we could all do together. Puzzle races, treasure hunts using a global positioning device, and cooking family heirloom recipes would bring us together and be our gifts to each other. In this relaxed atmosphere, without the pressure of gift giving, we could simply enjoy each other's company.

Charlie, with his quick wit and clever mind, could make every occasion a special event. Even getting a lasagna, which my sister Kathy had made and which had taken forever to thaw, from one cabin to the other became a memorable event when Charlie devised a way to bring the huge piping hot lasagna across the snow covered road on a sled with great fanfare.

Experiences like this throughout our marriage helped me to understand that Charlie's approach to gift giving was, in itself, an important gift to our family. The events surrounding his death would bring home to me even more clearly that his most precious gift to me was intangible.

Just what that gift was would take time to discover.

3

Playfulness

Inspired
By life's priorities
Every day
No matter what
Enjoy

Even though Charlie was a fun-loving and playful fellow and enjoyed putting drama to use for the sake of a few laughs, he was a very conventional and practical person. That he was a man of persistence and determination he demonstrated over and over again. Because he was so conventional and practical in many aspects of his personal and professional life, his dramatic playfulness seemed to be paradoxical, which made the situation even funnier. Often his dramatic playfulness was carried out in quiet and subtle ways with a persistence that flowed from his determination to keep from taking life too seriously. Yet he was a very serious person.

While Charlie made a career as a federal prosecutor, his undergraduate work had been in electrical engineering. But his experience at a summer job in the field of engineering quickly convinced him that he wouldn't be happy in this work and he went on to law school. In the law he would have an opportunity to meld his great love of language, his flair for drama, his great intelligence and quick mind with his persistent dedication to making the world a better place. After graduating from law school he embarked on a career prosecuting criminals and defending the federal government. He worked long hours and many weekends in order to leave no stone unturned in his investigations and to make all of his written and oral arguments absolutely convincing while defending the government's position. Yet he enjoyed taking time out of his own heavy schedule to mentor younger attorneys. However, in the midst of all this serious, time-consuming litigation he did make time to have fun. Later one of the younger attorneys in the office would tell me that his first impression after observing Charlie at a courtroom hearing was that he was much too serious. In time, he would find out otherwise.

14

Charlie's conventional and practical nature was quite apparent in his actions. He wore dark suits with white or pastel shirts and ties with simple patterns, along with loafers that he had bought a lifetime supply of when his favorite shoe store was going out of business. He came to a full stop at stop signs. In order to make sure he didn't miss taking his medications, he devised a system where each morning he put a pill he needed to take at lunchtime into his left pocket and then, when he had taken the pill, he would move the container to his right pocket. Each night after work, he would empty the change from his pockets and put it into a jar for later rolling. Our oldest daughter, Liz, tells how one of the enjoyable little rituals of growing up was sitting on the king-sized bed with her Dad sorting through the mountains of coins, looking for rare or special coins and then rolling the coins up in paper wrappers to redeem at the bank.

One December, our friend Dave wore a diamond earring to church. While Charlie was talking with Dave after Mass one Sunday morning, he discovered that the earring was held on by a magnet. When Charlie realized that he could wear an earring without getting his ear pierced, he decided he had to have one! He begged me to go shopping with him to help find him a similar pair of earrings. Once he bought the earrings he wore one to work every day, pretending to have had his ear pierced. He wore the diamond earring to every holiday party we attended during the Christmas season holding on to the story that he had had his ear pierced. His coworkers and our friends were astounded that Charlie, of all people, was wearing a diamond earring. He never let on at work or at the parties that this was a hoax. He carried the scheme off with quiet aplomb.

After wearing the earring to work for a week, his boss called him into his office to have a very serious talk about the fact that

Charlie could not wear the earring into the courtroom. Charlie agreed to follow the boss's dictate. However, he never let on that he really hadn't pierced his ear and that he was just having fun. When our family gathered at Blackwater Falls at Christmas time he continued to wear the earring, again never letting on until the end of the week, when he dramatically tore the earring off and shouted "Gotcha!"

After the holidays, Charlie continued his little joke at work. However, instead of the earring, he went to the office wearing a band-aid on his earlobe. That morning he had a serious conversation with one of the women about what to do about the infection he had gotten as a result of having his ear pierced. Eventually, everyone had a good laugh when he finally let on that the guy they knew as conventional and practical really hadn't had his ear pierced, he was just having a little fun.

So shortly after Charlie died, when I told the story of all the events surrounding Charlie's death to a gathering at my brother Jim's house, it wasn't surprising when my nephew Mike declared, "Just like Uncle Charlie!"

4

Mystery

In present time I hear
The morning sounds of birds
Commingling with the sounds of the universe

In morning stillness I hear
Beyond the chirping and the singing
The call of the universe

In present time I hear
Eternity

In the months preceding Charlie's death, he had difficulty eating and he was losing weight. We went from doctor to doctor in search of a diagnosis. When the diagnosis did come it was grim–metastatic lung cancer with a prognosis of average life expectancy of four months. A young British doctor recommended no treatment. He encouraged Charlie, saying, "Go home and enjoy the little time you have left of life." After listening to this doctor, Charlie bravely accepted what he already suspected–that his life was to be cut short. Both of us were prepared to take on the challenge of facing his death directly and making the most of our time together. But, then, a specialist at a renowned hospital in Baltimore suggested chemotherapy; however, he dawdled before giving us a referral. When we finally did get to an oncologist, he suggested that we go to a doctor closer to home, delaying the start of treatment even longer. About that time our internist, who had guided Charlie and me through several serious illnesses since we were married, encouraged him to take chemotherapy, saying, "I had a patient whose cancer was as advanced as yours. Chemotherapy gave her ten good years." So Charlie began treatment.

Just before he started taking chemotherapy, a tumor behind his eye began to cause double vision and Charlie lost his ability to read. With his favorite pastime taken away, he decided to spend the time listening to all the CDs we owned. While the classical music, show tunes and pop music filled the house with a sense of normalcy, the tension between accepting what seemed inevitable–his death–and having treatment to keep him alive, grew. Charlie's condition continued to deteriorate.

Time was ticking away and we were anxious and confused. He continued with treatment, and I continued to encourage him.

18

However, when he couldn't eat, I got discouraged and angry. Living between the hope for life through medical treatment and the growing realization that Charlie's life force was waning, depleted our emotional reserves. It was a difficult time. We argued. As long as he was still taking treatment, I wanted him to work harder at living. He seemed to know that he wouldn't get well, but he was unable to express this to me, or, more than likely, it was I who was unable to hear him. I wanted him to live.

After the diagnosis, when I talked with friends and family, I asked them to pray for us, saying "We need a miracle." Each time I asked them to pray I suspended a fear that Charlie's condition had deteriorated to the point that nothing could help. I never said, "Pray for a miracle." because the situation appeared to be hopeless. I doubted that a miracle could happen to us. If miracles happened, they happened to more faith-filled persons. I could never suspend my doubt to specifically ask God for a miracle.

I prayed a different kind of prayer, which brought me peace. I prayed by being with Charlie, by keeping him comfortable, by Massaging his body. I prayed by telling him that he was a good husband and that I loved him. "Thank you for being my husband," I told him again and again as I wanted him to know how grateful I was for his presence in my life. At night we fell asleep lying on our backs next to each other just like the first night we had met with my right hand resting in his left hand. We awoke each morning in the same position.

Each evening I massaged his body with a lightly fragrant cream that my friend Jean had brought back from the Holy Land. I moved my hands across Charlie's chest and arms, then his lower body, finally reaching his legs and feet. With the delicate lotion, I embraced him as completely and as gently as I could, savoring each moment and each sensation of touching and holding his frail

19

and helpless body. His faint heart beat visibly in his bony chest. Charlie's life was ebbing with each shallow breath. It was a special time and a holy time that my daughters and I shared with Charlie. Liz, who was living in San Diego, Katie who was in North Carolina, and Laura who was in Boston, had taken turns coming home during the summer to spend time with Charlie. But when it became apparent that his death was imminent, they all left their work to help care for him.

On a comfortably warm and quiet Monday evening in August, I Massaged Charlie's upper body. When I reached his legs I was unable to go on. I didn't Massage his feet as I had each night. I went to bed lying next to him. I didn't hold his hand.

At 2:30 in the morning, I awoke from a deep sleep in a kind of stupor. Unaware of my surroundings and the life and death situation Charlie and I were involved in at the moment, I went to the bathroom. As I opened the bathroom door to go back to bed, Charlie's still form lying in bed brought me to my senses and I remembered what was happening. I went to his side. His chest was still. I could see that he wasn't breathing, but I wasn't immediately concerned as there had been long pauses between his breaths in the preceding days. When I noticed that I couldn't see his heart beating, I put my hand on his chest. His heart was still. Feeling no heartbeat, I thought to myself, "He's gone." Then in a gesture of farewell, I placed my hand on the top of his head to say, "Goodbye."

As I rested my hand on his head, I suddenly knew with absolute certainty that Charlie was still alive. The awareness that he was still present was so strong that I never thought to question it. I ran through the house to wake our two daughters, Liz and Laura, who were at home that night, saying to them, "Dad is dying now. Do you want to be with him when he leaves?" The three of us ran to

20

be with him. Just as we seated ourselves at his bedside ready to remain in his presence while he left us, **the lights went out**.

Startled by the loss of electric power on a calm, quiet night, we sat in the dark expecting the lights to flicker back on. After a few moments we realized the power would not return and we scurried about the house gathering candles. We lit several candles and then when we returned our attention to Charlie it was apparent that he was gone. Distracted by the unexpected loss of electricity, we hadn't noticed when he left us.

The silence of early morning surrounded us as we sat with Charlie in the candlelight. I felt the warmth as it left his still body. After a time I phoned Charlie's sister, Marian, and invited her and her daughter, Kathryn, to join us in saying good-bye to Charlie, our beloved husband, father, brother and uncle. As they drove through the neighborhood to join Liz and Laura and me they noticed that the street lights were out. They sat with us at Charlie's side. As dawn overcame darkness, a peacefulness, which bathed us in its light, filled the room and touched our souls.

Our neighborhood was without power for four hours that morning. There was no explanation for the interruption of electrical service on a calm and balmy night in the middle of August. When the power did return at 6:30 am, Darrell, who was the last friend to visit with Charlie, reported, "We were awakened by all the appliances in the house coming on at once."

The timing of the electrical outage at the precise moment that the three of us settled into the room to be with Charlie as he left this life gave us the opportunity to savor these last peace-filled moments with Charlie as his spirit left. The coincidence of these two events felt important and meaningful, but at the time I hadn't fully understood what was happening.

In the following days, weeks, and months I was comforted by the memory of our time together in the glow of candlelight surrounding us and Charlie's still body. But I would have both comforting and unsettling experiences over the next few years before I would understand what was happening when the lights went out.

5

Synchronicity

Beyond the rules of nature
I fly
You hover
We are beyond the rules of nature
If we let go

The tension tickled down to our toes. With our eyes focused on the teacher sitting at the old upright piano, an electric energy pulsed between my fifth grade classmates and our enthusiastic teacher. We rose to her challenge. Allowing the rhythm of the song that mimicked the tick-tocking of a clock to lead us, we sang:

> My grandfather's clock was too large for the shelf so it stood ninety years on the floor.
> It was taller by half than the old man himself though it weighed not a pennyweight more.
> It was bought on the morn of the day that he was born and was always his treasure and pride

I felt the ticking of the big clock all through my body as we reached the next line:

> But it stopp'd short - - - -

The teacher's hands jumped off the piano keys indicating a full measure of silence. The challenge of creating a unison silence captured our attention and all twenty-five of us tried to be totally silent. It didn't always work. Sometimes a syllable hung over or came too soon and then an embarrassed giggle erupted. Over and over again we practiced, never tiring of working together to get it just right. When the moment of complete silence filled the room, the teacher's beaming face thrilled us only half as much as the satisfaction and sense of mastery which we felt in every cell of our ten year-old bodies. Following the lead of her hand held high above the piano, our voices continued crisply:

24

Never-to-go-again-when-the

Then in a singsongy way we sang:

Old.   Man.   died.

Pride puffed out our chests as we renewed the syncopated rhythm:

Ninety years without slumbering, tick, tock, tick, tock
His life seconds numbering, tick, tock, tick, tock

Then again:

But it stopp'd short - - - - never-to-go-again-when-the
Old.   Man.   died.

Just a child's song with silly lyrics; I never imagined that the events it described had ever happened. I never heard of a real life story when a clock stopped when someone died.

When I was a little girl my mother told me the story of the temple curtain being torn in two when Jesus died. "At 12 o'clock the sun stopped shining and darkness covered the whole country till three o'clock when the curtain hanging in the temple was torn in two." It was easy to believe. Of course, spectacular events had happened when Jesus died. Jesus was no ordinary person. He was the Son of God.

Only once had I heard of a meaningful event happening when someone died. My friend Mimi, was awakened in the middle of the night by the urgent pecking of a bird on the glass pane of her bedroom window. Then in the very next moment, her phone rang.

It was the nurse caring for her mother 2000 miles away in Arizona, calling to tell Mimi that her mother had just died. The bird's tapping at the precise moment of her mother's death was meaningful to Mimi. She believed that the bird signaled her mother's passing from this life to the next.

When the lights went out when Charlie died, a peacefulness descended upon me. As we sat with his still body I felt a sense of safety and security. I had no fear. I knew that something beautiful, something mysterious, something wonderful had happened at the moment of his death but I found the beauty, mystery, and wonder difficult to articulate. A graced serenity surrounded me through the days of the wake and funeral and followed me into the succeeding weeks.

After the funeral, in an attempt to communicate all that was in my heart, I gave a candle to everyone whose love and prayers had sustained our family during the last months of Charlie's life. A candle seemed an appropriate gift, not only because it symbolized the light of Christ and the promise of eternal life, but also because the warmth and glow of the candle's flame spoke of the power of the love burning in my heart, my love for Charlie, and his love for me. A candle also told the literal story of the lights going out when Charlie died, so it seemed a perfect way to express in a tangible way the beauty, mystery, and wonder that had accompanied the moment of Charlie's death. Little did I know that the candles given in gratitude and with a sense of awe would foreshadow future events.

In the days immediately after Charlie's death, I told the story of the lights going out at the moment of his death over and over again. I assumed that people would appreciate the awe I experienced in the synchronicity of the two events. But, a year later, I discovered that my friend Cathy had not understood that the lights had literally gone out when Charlie died. Because she thought I was speaking metaphorically when I said, "The lights went out when Charlie died," she didn't appreciate the sense of wonder that I was attempting to convey in giving her a candle. She had difficulty understanding what actually happened because in the retelling of the story I was afraid to make my message clear. I spoke without conviction. I sounded vague. I had allowed my doubt to overcome my belief in the miraculous nature of the events surrounding Charlie's death.

Of these things I am certain. Charlie was alive when I put my hand on his head. The lights went out the moment Charlie's spirit left his body. And the lyrics of the silly children's song about the clock stopping when the old man died are grounded in reality.

I'm also certain that Charlie still lives. I feel his presence. I know he is with me. Charlie is with me wherever I am. I came to this realization slowly, after a series of seemingly inconsequential events. The first one would happen at Charlie's gravesite a few days after his burial.

6

Significance

A minute lost from
Eternity
Is captured in a
Feather
From a bird's wing

Charlie and I have three daughters. During Charlie's last summer they each took time from their work to come home and be with him. In the last weeks all three of them were at home helping to care for him. Liz and Laura were with me in the bedroom with Charlie when the lights went out as Charlie left this life. Katie wasn't at home the night that Charlie died.

In the spring and summer of 1995 Katie hiked the Appalachian Trail from Georgia to Maine. Bursting with pride about her endeavor, Charlie had posted a map of the trail in his office and kept his co-workers aware of her progress by marking the dates and her location along the trail. After her adventure on the trail, Katie became involved in trail maintenance and repair and at the time of Charlie's last illness, she was at a work camp in North Carolina. During the summer she came home to visit periodically, but when it became apparent that Charlie's time was coming to an end, she left the work camp to help care for him. She understood the workings of the mechanical equipment and kept it running smoothly. While the breathing apparatus hummed, she spent hours sitting on the other side of our king-sized bed being attentive to Charlie in her quiet way. Charlie wasn't able to talk and, of all of us, Katie was the most comfortable with silence.

On a Monday morning in mid-August, with the early morning sun streaming through the kitchen window, Katie asked me, "Do you think Dad will die today?" She wanted to be with him when he died, but it was the last day of work camp and she hoped to say good-bye to her friends and pick up her belongings.

I knew in my heart that Charlie couldn't last much longer. A week earlier the hospice nurse had advised me that death could come momentarily. Yet he continued to cling to life. Each day I swabbed Charlie's mouth with cool water and he swallowed a few drops. I wondered how long he could live with so little nourishment. The pauses between his breaths grew and he became less responsive, yet the fragile thread of life held. So in response to Katie's question I said, "We have no way of knowing when Dad will die. You've been faithful caring for him and sometimes we have to take care of our own needs." Katie decided to leave. She planned to return the following day.

The next morning when I called her at work camp to tell her of Charlie's death during the night, she was heartbroken. There was little I could do but listen to her cries of sadness and disappointment. Friends drove her home that day. When she arrived we told her the story of the lights going out when Charlie died and about the peacefulness we had experienced in the candlelight as his spirit left.

Surrounded by friends and family during the days of Charlie's wake, funeral, and burial, I was comforted by their love and their presence. This and the sense of peacefulness I experienced as Charlie's spirit left, combined to strengthen me.

However, after we had said our good-byes to the last out-of-town relative and when my daughters and I were left alone, the emptiness created by Charlie's absence intensified. The four of us missed Charlie and we wondered how to manage without his lively, fun-loving presence. Liz, Laura, and I went about the days managing to find joy in living in spite of our sadness, but Katie moped around the house and said little. She responded to none of our efforts to comfort her and remained uncommunicative except for a sullen grumpiness. I worried about Katie, yet I understood there was little I could do to help her through her grief and disappointment. I couldn't change the facts. Although she had been faithful in caring for her Dad, she hadn't been with him and with us in that very special moment when Charlie left us.

A tense and unhealthy atmosphere descended upon the household. Minutes seemed like hours. We were all on edge. I knew I had the strength to cope with Charlie's death, but I wasn't certain that I could help Katie through her distress. Worst of all, I feared that her behavior would have an isolating effect upon all of us. As I struggled with ideas about how to get us through the day, suddenly, I voiced an inspiration. "Let's go to the cemetery together." Everyone agreed to go. When we arrived at the cemetery I placed a big blanket on the grass under the craggy white pine tree that shaded the mound of wilting flowers on Charlie's grave. Liz, Laura and I lay down on the blanket in quiet reflection.

Katie went off by herself, wandering down the paths and through the grassy areas around the gravestones. After some time, our reverie on the blanket was broken as Katie approached. A broad smile flashed across her face and she held her hands cupped around something. Extending her arms to show us the tiny, pale gray, down feather cradled in her hands, she declared "An angel's wing feather." She described how it had fallen from the sky and came to rest in her hands.

With Katie's declaration, I remembered that I had asked Charlie to tell me when the angels came for him. I was beginning to understand the loss of light when Charlie died and our peacefulness in the candlelight. Still, I told no one. The doubting part of me held my tongue tight.

Later Katie told me, "It was good that I wasn't home when Dad died. I would have been so upset that you wouldn't have been able to enjoy the peacefulness in the candlelight." I also believe her absence made it easier for Charlie to leave. Understanding her sensitive nature and not wanting to hurt her, he slipped away when she was gone for the day.

32

After Charlie's death, my thoughts drifted to him frequently throughout the day. I managed to stay focused at work, but during other daily activities such as shopping, showering, cleaning, meditating, and swimming, memories of Charlie and of his last days flooded through my mind. I noticed when I was thinking of him when I was outside, wandering though the garden, hiking in the woods, or walking through the neighborhood or on the path to my office door, I was often drawn out of my reverie by a feather that lay directly in my path. Because the feathers reminded me of Katie's angel wing feather and renewed my faith in Charlie's continued presence in my life, I picked up each feather and brought it home with me. The feathers reminded me of the peacefulness at the moment of Charlie's death. When I doubted that Charlie's spirit still lived, when I doubted that he was still present in my life, the feathers kept my doubt contained. When I had enough feathers, large, dark ones, small, colorful ones, and tiny, soft down feathers, I made a wreath of them.

As I sit at my desk writing this story, the wreath hangs on the wall behind me. With the wreath of feathers over my shoulder I feel Charlie's presence and his encouragement to persist even when self-doubt overwhelms me. But in the midst of my conviction that Charlie is still with me, at times I find myself doubting. This uncertainty lurked at the edges of my psyche even when continuing coincidences involving light and feathers renewed my faith in Charlie's presence.

.

7

Skepticism

On a tee shirt
"Plays well with others"
That you did
And now you are playing with me
For fun
For real?

In the first weeks after Charlie's death, each time I went to Sunday Mass, one of the two candles on the altar caught my attention when it began to flicker. Then, when the liturgy was over, I would notice that that candle's flame had gone out while the other one remained lighted. I enjoyed this simple confirmation of Charlie's continued presence in my life and the wonder associated with the events surrounding his death. In those early days after Charlie's death, I often felt his presence palpably over my right shoulder, and in those moments at church when I noticed a candle flickering, my awareness of his presence was heightened and intensified.

I shared these comforting moments with my family and with my closest friends. Sharing the awe I experienced helped me to overcome any doubt about the wonder of these little miracles. But I also needed others to confirm for me the importance of these signs. Several times when I told the story to a priest, tears would come to his eyes and I found his tears reaffirming of the mystery. But while I told the story with a certainty, I also experienced a fearfulness associated with broadcasting my belief that something mysterious and meaningful was happening in each of these little events. After all, the electricity going out and a candle flame extinguishing itself are ordinary events that happen every day. Could it be that these particular events that were happening to me were just ordinary events? Or were they little miracles? The doubting part of me countered my belief in the mysterious and miraculous nature of these coincidences by telling me, "It is probably the same candle that goes out each week and it's probably got a defective wick."

Then, about a month after Charlie's death, friends arranged for a Saturday morning Mass at our church to remember him. As we sat in the pew together all the light bulbs in a large brass chandelier above the baptismal font to the right of the altar began to flicker. We looked at each other with a knowing glance, thinking of the lights going out when Charlie died and wondering if this was another sign that Charlie was with us. The flickering continued through the Mass. Then, at the very moment the priest finished saying, "The Mass is over. Go in peace," all the lights in the church went out with an abrupt "pfffst." We were amazed! Here was another wonderful confirmation that Charlie is still with us!

Fortunately for me, this event was witnessed not just by me and our friends, Arlene and David, who also knew that the electricity had gone out the morning of Charlie's death, but also by another friend, Bob, who had been out of town and hadn't known that Charlie had died. We shared with Bob the story and the wonder of the events associated with Charlie's death. Bob countered any doubt I had about what we had experienced, when he assured us that, yes, indeed, the lights had been flickering during the Mass.

So why do I have such difficulty believing my own eyes? Why am I such a doubter? Why do I continually need the reassurance of others in order to sustain my faith? I know why. When I look back to my own childhood, I see the reasons why.

8

History

You may not be in my life
But your story
And my story
Are the same story
And a million years won't change that

A small picture in a narrow gold frame hung on the wall of the bedroom I shared with my sister Kathy when we were little. In the picture a guardian angel with wings spread wide hovers over a little boy and girl as they travel across a rickety bridge over a deep, dark ravine. I am sure the picture was meant to comfort little children who were afraid of the dark and of falling asleep, but it had the opposite effect on me. It scared me.

I looked at the bridge and its missing planks and saw hidden terror below in the dark swirling waters. The presence of the angel didn't allay my fears. In my little girl's mind I saw the beautiful children in the picture, the little girl with flowing wavy blond hair and the handsome boy, as good children and reasoned that the guardian angel protected good children. I was a tall, skinny kid with the straightest of brown hair and I wondered if the angel protected children who weren't good all the time. Would she protect me since I wasn't always a good girl? Sometimes I was disobedient and angry and fought with my sister and brothers. I doubted that the angel protected children who were bad. How could the angel protect me?

My mother and father, while totally dedicated to care of their six little children–all of us being born before I was seven–had many arguments when we were growing up. On the surface the arguments were about money. Where did the money go? How much money to give to the church? How much money to spend on doll carriages for my sister and me? I was the oldest and a sensitive, responsible child troubled by the discord between my parents. I thought it was my responsibility to reconcile their differences and keep the peace. While the arguments between my parents took on many manifestations seemingly related to money, with the wisdom of years, I have been able to discern that the underlying theme of the arguments was the tension between faith and doubt. My mother put her faith in God so completely and absolutely that she allowed herself to relinquish any practicality. She bought my sister and me large, sturdy, and beautiful but expensive doll carriages when simple ones might have sufficed to make us happy. My father, on the other hand, was a very practical person. He came from a family that had abandoned the church when his father's first wife died because, as family lore told us, he did not have enough money to give a priest to say a funeral Mass for her. Not only had the family given up their faith in the church but they also disparaged those who were believers. My father called my mother's faith "hocus-pocus." It has taken me many years to recognize that, when my father belittled my mother's faith with those words, he was merely asking her to be more practical.

My parent's arguments about money masked the fact that they were struggling with the issue of doubt and faith. Underlying their arguments about money were difficult questions about the implications of faith. Did budgeting mean that you didn't have faith that God would provide? Did having faith that God would provide mean that being realistic and practical weren't important? My father saw my mother's convictions as a barrier to practicality. My mother saw my father's practicality as a threat to her faith.

As time went on their stances became rigid and a righteousness developed in each of them about their own ways of perceiving the world. They moved to extreme positions that polarized them so that they could not listen to each other's concerns in order to come to a meeting of the minds. Unable to recognize that faith and doubt can coexist, there was little room for compromise in their relationship.

Faith and doubt need to co-exist in order to allow dialogue to develop.

41

Without openness to dialogue, we run the risk of becoming righteous and ultimately fanatical. When we are righteous we reduce all the mysteries of life and of the world to the way we comprehend reality. Righteousness takes all the complexity out of life and reduces it to our own rigid beliefs about how things are. Our own faith, our own beliefs become the only way to make sense of reality. Such rigidity is helpful because it reduces anxiety by diminishing the wondrous complexity of life to simply our own way of seeing reality. But, unrestrained, this way of making sense of the world leads ultimately to fanaticism. That fanaticism allows us to dismiss and reject completely any world view which is not congruent with our own.

Faith and doubt are not contradictory, for one contains elements of the other. Professing one does not negate the other, for they complement one another. They are yin and yang. One is incomplete without the other; one has no meaning without the other.

As a little girl who wanted to please each of my parents, I was torn between embracing their contradictory approaches to life. If I had faith I was disloyal to my father. If I took my father's doubting approach I was disloyal to my mother. I never doubted their love for me, but growing up in this environment was confusing. I was guilty no matter what I did. I didn't have a word for the feelings I experienced so I couldn't tell anyone about it. The guilt lay hidden in the midst of confusing thoughts and feelings and went underground. I became anxious. Anxious about what? I didn't know. I remember hearing people talk about free-floating anxiety and wondering what those words meant. I didn't understand what they were talking about, but I remembered the words. They were talking about what I was experiencing.

I was afraid to speak up. I was caught in the midst of a terrible dilemma–how to keep everyone happy and be true to myself. It was a frightening challenge for a little girl to navigate. I fell into the trap and I lost myself. I remember the day it happened.

One day when I was about nine, the family visited the monastery where my mother's sister, my godmother, Rita, lived as a cloistered nun. At the end of our visit, as I was buttoning the big, brown buttons of my bulky, beige coat, Aunt Rita motioned to me from behind the black wire grill that separated her and the other cloistered nuns from their visitors. Into my ear she whispered, "I am praying that your father becomes a Catholic." I wanted to scream out, "He's a good person even if he isn't a Catholic. He doesn't need to be Catholic." Of course, I didn't say a word.

My parents continued this battle over faith and doubt all their lives. My father never went to church with us except for specials occasions such as first communions, confirmations, and weddings. But he surprised us by embracing the Catholic Church after my mother's death. He never did tell us what caused him to embrace the faith and let go of his doubt. Perhaps without my mother's opposition to his doubt it was easier for faith to grow even in the midst of his own doubt.

Both my mother and father are gone now, but their legacy still lives on in me. I am torn between giving myself over to total faith or hanging onto my doubt. I am a faith-filled person, but at the same time I am a rational being and that part of me, encouraged by my father, is a skeptic to the core. This internal conflict between faith and doubt has been intensified and brought to the surface by the circumstances surrounding Charlie's death. The anxiety and guilt around the issues that I've carried with me since childhood have lain hidden in the deep recesses of my psyche and have only recently become xposed to the light of day.

Reconciling the skeptical and the faith-filled parts of me as I dealt with the mysterious coincidences related to Charlie's death would bring me a new freedom, the freedom to be more myself.

Doubt, with its roots deep in my early childhood, hovers over me just as surely as the broad wings of the guardian angel hover over the little children crossing the bridge. But the story does not end here. Without the repeated confirmation of faith in the events that followed, most likely I would not have had the courage to overcome the skeptic in me to tell the story of *Charlie's Gift*.

9

Presence

In the cathedral of my heart
Are vast and empty spaces
Where the echoing sounds of the night's stillness
Assure me of your presence

Pauline Dotzler Flynn

The first year after the death of a spouse is a year of profound transitions, transitions that occur on many levels–practical, psychological, and spiritual. The practical transitions demand attention because the organization of our society requires that they be made. For example, the Department of Motor Vehicles rejected my application for the renewal of my automobile registration. Because the car had been jointly owned by Charlie and me, the DMV required that I take Charlie's name off the title before it would renew the registration. Somehow the DMV knew that he was deceased.

As practical concerns are addressed, psychological and spiritual transitions are also happening, but often with less notice and sometimes less consciously. So, as the year after Charlie's death was coming to a close, I had taken care of most of the practical matters, but I was still dealing with the psychological and spiritual issues. Every night I went to bed alone, every time I cooked dinner for myself and sat at the dining room table eating alone, or went to church alone, I was making psychological adjustments and coming to grips with the reality that Charlie was not in my everyday life any longer.

When the oven wouldn't work and I had to decide whether to repair it or buy a new stove, I was faced with the realization that I couldn't turn to Charlie to help me make practical decisions. When the car was giving me problems, I had to decide by myself what kind of new car to buy. I wasn't accustomed to making such decisions alone. Big decisions liking buying a new car were always made after consultation with each other. As I met each of these challenges I was learning how to manage life as a single woman and psychologically making adjustments to my new status.

This new independence was frightening at times. At other times it felt heady. Sometimes, I found myself making small and major

46

decisions that would have been in direct opposition to what Charlie would have done. For example, I purchased a new refrigerator even though the old one wasn't broken, a decision Charlie's frugality never would have tolerated. I also changed the way I invested money, from his very conservative approach to a more aggressive approach.

Painful as it was, I was learning how to reconstruct my life as a single woman, finding a balance between being alone with my grief and sharing it with friends and family. I was managing to take care of the household and create a stimulating social life. I felt a growing confidence that I could manage my life. At times I actually enjoyed my independence; however, I panicked at the thought of vacationing alone.

In the quiet desperation that I experienced when I imagined traveling without Charlie, my thoughts turned to my daughters. I decided I wanted to share with them the wondrous moments Charlie and I had had on our many vacations. Taking them to the places that Charlie and I had enjoyed would be a way to keep Charlie alive in my memory and in theirs. It was also a step in learning to cope with being a single woman again after 30 years of marriage.

Just two years before he died, Charlie and I had discovered the mysterious beauty of the desert east of San Diego. Charlie hated the cold, so we researched weather maps looking for an area of the country that had the highest average temperatures in winter. We climbed to the top of the Kelso Dunes and then, acting like kids we laughed as the sand made a humming noise as we slid down the dunes. While camping on the shores of the Salton Sea we gloried in a spectacular sunset while a brilliant vermilion glow surrounded us and the dark forms of the mountains were reflected in the water of the great salty sea. In the quiet of the vast empty spaces of Death Valley we felt a closeness to each other and to the barren landscape as we hiked across its expansive salt flats.

It was during this trip that Charlie and I fell in love with the landscape at Joshua Tree National Park. We arrived at the camping area at dusk when campfires were burning and lanterns were casting a glow in the fading light. While pitching our tent in the dark we could hear the echoing sounds of kids' voices coming from the midst of the huge, mysterious shapes surrounding the campsite. We went to sleep wondering about the surrounding landscape. At morning's first light, while the night's stillness hung over the campground, we unzipped the tent and were greeted by a surprising sight. We were surrounded on all sides by magnificent boulders. Our campsite was barely larger than the tent itself and from the campsite boulders rose in all directions, some standing erect in the early light, others lying on their sides. Some were so large they appeared to soar straight into the heavens. Smaller ones were piled on top of larger ones. We were camped in a boulder cathedral! In the early morning light the cathedral walls were a muted yellow-orange and the soft, clear blue of the sky its vaulted ceiling. A silent awe filled our hearts.

So, the first winter after Charlie was gone, my daughters and I planned a vacation together in southern California. After joining Liz at her apartment in San Diego, the four of us drove from the city to explore the desert that lies to the east. The weather was cold, windy, and rainy. We had planned to camp, but given the nasty weather, we decided that staying at motels with hot tubs would be a preferable substitute for our usual family camping trip.

After a few nights we headed toward Joshua Tree National Park because I wanted to share with them the special experience that Charlie and I had together while camping there on one of our last vacations together. When we arrived at the park it was important to me to show the girls the exact location where Charlie and I had camped. I wanted them to see the precise spot where Charlie and I had fallen in love with this awe-inspiring beauty. Enduring the damp chill of the desert air, the four of us climbed around the sandy-orange boulders surrounding the campsites until we came to the campsite where Charlie and I had spent the night. Just as I exclaimed, "This is it!" snowflakes fell in a flurry around us and the swirling wind enfolded us with a mist of whiteness. Charlie was with us! We could feel his presence. Snowflakes in the biting wind melted any doubt I had about the fact that Charlie was still with us. (Two winters later, as I finished writing this paragraph, I looked up from my computer to see that it had begun to snow.)

Here was another confirmation! How could I continue to doubt when some new experience would renew my faith in Charlie's continued presence?

10

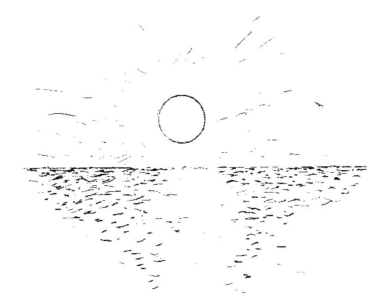

Comfort

Sunlight skims across the ocean
From where earth meets sky
From horizon to the shore
Shining on me
Where ever
I stand

As the first year after Charlie's death wore on, I wondered about how I could manage future vacations. I still couldn't imagine facing the adventure of a solo trip, so I developed a plan to give each of my daughters a trip for her birthday. For Laura's birthday I invited her to come to the Cayman Islands with me. I chose Grand Cayman because I didn't feel adventurous enough to go someplace I hadn't been before. Charlie and I had discovered Grand Cayman on our honeymoon. We had found the pure white sands and the crystal blue water of its Seven Mile Beach enchanting.

When we returned to Grand Cayman to celebrate our anniversary 20 years later, Charlie and I discovered Smith's Cove. Smith's Cove is a quiet little beach enclosed on two sides by a rocky ledge. It is a perfect place for swimming and snorkeling. After snorkeling in the calm, clear waters and enjoying the colorful, tropical fish and coral formations under a bright blue sky, Charlie and I left to continue exploring the island. On our return trip, as we passed the Cove, a storm was approaching. Much to our surprise the placid little alcove had been transformed. The translucent aqua water was being churned by a fierce wind that dashed the water against the gray-black rocks and hurled a foamy white spray up into the now dark, cloud-laden sky. Charlie waited as I took a photo of the stormy scene that spoke to me of the uncertainty of life—calm one moment, treacherous the next. Yet, in the clarity of the turquoise water and the magnificence of foamy spray flying into the air, I saw beauty in the turmoil and knew that safety and security can exist even in the midst of terror. This picture hangs in my office as a symbol of hope during the stormy times in one's life. I believe the scene encourages my clients to embrace the deep peace within themselves even while life is full of turmoil.

As soon as Laura and I arrived on Grand Cayman I wanted to show her Smith's Cove. So, after settling in to our condo, Laura and I drove to Smith's Cove to go snorkeling. While I was examining the coral formations through my snorkel mask, I could see out the corner of my eye a disturbance in the water and a long stream of bubbles. Looking in that direction I watched Laura as she dove to the bottom. When she surfaced she had a broad grin across her face and delight in her eyes. Holding up a five dollar bill Cayman, she declared, "Dad would be proud of me." Charlie, a competitive swimmer and lifeguard while he was in college, had taught Laura to swim and dive and indeed he would have been proud of her. We celebrated Charlie's continuing presence in our lives with Laura treating me to a drink and candy bar with her newfound five dollar bill.

Being with my daughters is always a way to feel Charlie's presence. I am aware that he lives in each one of them in some way. It is in moments together with them that I know that we are still a family—me, Charlie, Liz, Katie, and Laura. Being with them in the special places that Charlie and I enjoyed together and sharing with them the beauty and the sense of awe and connectedness to all of life that we experienced has a way of making his presence felt even more intensely so that I know he still lives, not just in memory, but in reality.

11

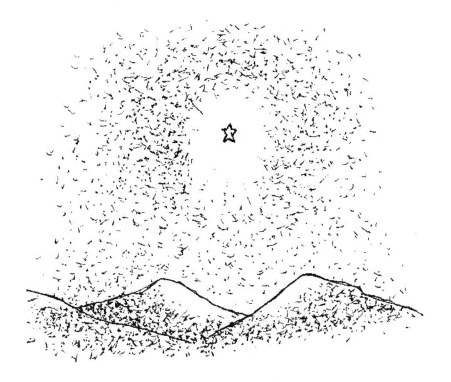

Appreciation

A breath away from eternity
A star to show the way
You light the way
A beacon for me

I n July, almost a year after Charlie's death, I decided that I wanted to celebrate his birthday. It seemed too painful to let the day go by without commemorating it in some way. But I also knew I would need the help of my family and friends to get through the day.

So I spent some time thinking of an appropriate way to celebrate his life that would honor his unique characteristics and his values.

Charlie was a down-to-earth guy who liked simple food and simple fun. He wasn't a gourmet and had no interest in becoming one. Even when his co-workers touted the superiority of microbrews, all he wanted was a Millers High Life. He had been an inveterate game player ever since he was a child and he never outgrew his love of games. Word games were his favorites, especially Scrabble and Upwords. Pictionary and Charades were his favorite party games. He loved winning and while he was playing he never took his mind off winning. He didn't lose often, but when he did, he wasn't a sore loser. What he loved was the mental challenge that games presented and the engagement with others in the pursuit of lighthearted fun.

So after contemplating these unique characteristics of Charlie's personality, I decided to invite family and friends to play games in his memory on his birthday. I concluded that Charlie's simplicity was one of his greatest gifts to me and to our family. By taking time to play games and drink beer together, we could honor him and still keep learning from him. Playing games is a way to keep Charlie's spirit alive in our family, so we ate pizza, drank beer, and played Pictionary. It was a joyful celebration of Charlie's life and his legacy. The birthday party allowed us to hold on to Charlie's presence in the midst of his absence.

56

Having managed to survive, and much to my surprise, actually enjoy, celebrating Charlie's first birthday in his absence, the next challenge facing me was the first anniversary of his death less than a month after his birthday. It seemed natural to have a Mass said for him on that day, which I did. But I also felt the need to let my friends and family know how helpful they had been to me during the first year of intense mourning by giving each of them a gift. With this gift I wanted to commemorate the very special events associated with his death.

So to celebrate the one-year anniversary of Charlie's death, I gave a second candle to my friends and family members in continuing appreciation for their emotional support as I navigated the profound transitions that I needed to make as a result of losing my spouse of 30 years. The candles were a thank you for helping me mourn the loss of Charlie and for the comfort my friends and family provided when they listened to me recount over and over again memories of Charlie and the stories of his last illness, his last days, and his death. The candles were also given in appreciation for the memories of Charlie which people had shared with me about the impact that Charlie had had in their lives.

The simple little gift of a candle held much meaning for me. In the act of giving the candles I relived the graced moment of Charlie's leaving, and I was soothed by the memory. The candles were a way of saying thank you to Charlie for his life and they provided a way for me to keep Charlie's spirit alive in me and in all the people who are important to me and to him.

The candles helped to light the way into the darkness that lay ahead in the uncertainty of the future. The light of each candle reassured me of Charlie's presence in my life in the midst of the anxiety about how to manage my new life without him.

57

Pauline Dotzler Flynn

With the help of others, I had navigated the first year after Charlie's death. There still remained challenges to face as I made the transition to accepting life as a single woman.

I was discovering that my greatest personal challenge would be to integrate the believing and doubting parts of myself.

12

Reassurance

A sliver of moon
And a tiny star
Herald the end of the day
And bless me
As the night begins

People who have lost a loved one often have dreams in which the loved one appears. Since people find the appearance of the deceased in dreams very comforting, I longed to have Charlie come to me in a dream. I yearned to see him again, even if it was only in a dream.

It was a long time before Charlie appeared in my dreams. In fact, it was a year and half after he died before I had my first dream in which he appeared. On Saint Patrick's Day morning, I awoke remembering:

> *I am surrounded by friends and family. We are all waiting for Charlie when he appears on a raised platform in front of us. We cannot approach him since the platform separates us from him. I feel the distance between us, yet it isn't intimidating because I can see Charlie very clearly. He is radiant. His face is beaming. In the big smile that lights up his face I know that he is happy to see us.*
>
> *His face is youthful and clean-shaven (in life he always sported a mustache and sometimes a beard as well). His tall and lanky frame is clothed in monk's robes. I am puzzling over his monk's clothing when I suddenly I realize that the monk's garb makes sense since he has been on retreat.*

The dream comforted me. I felt the safety of Charlie's presence although there was a distance separating us. I couldn't reach out and touch him, yet I experienced the intensity of the connection between us. I was reassured that Charlie still loves me and our family and friends from his new place in heaven.

I laugh a little when I think that maybe Charlie in heaven is surprised to discover how connected we still are. As a young bride I remember lying together in our big king-sized bed one night just before falling asleep. Even after just a few years as husband and wife, I was feeling so connected to him that I couldn't imagine us ever being separated, not even by death. So I asked him, "Do you think we'll still be married in heaven?" He simply answered, "No." His response settled the question. I doubted my own intuitive knowledge. I wanted him to believe as I did. But I could not persuade him that making the leap from the intensity of my feeling of our interconnectedness to believing that our marriage was an everlasting reality was rational.

Now when I look back on that particular moment, I see again how I allowed the tension between faith and doubt to be resolved in favor of doubt. Without Charlie's agreement with me, I didn't have the reassurance I needed to believe my own experience. I needed his affirmation of my belief in order to hold on to my faith in my own experience.

The struggle for dominance by the doubting part of me means that the faith-filled part of me needs continual reassurance that comes only from the agreement of others. As a consequence, the believing part of me is confined to asking questions. It doesn't have the courage to assert itself with direct statements. Otherwise, I would have said to Charlie, "I feel so connected to you that I believe we will be connected to each other even after we die."

When he lay dying, if I had been able to hold my doubting self in check, I would have made a direct request, "Please let me know when the angels come for you." Instead, I asked him, "Will you tell me when the angels come for you?"

I am beginning to understand that I must voice both my faith and my doubt if I am to make the story of circumstances surrounding Charlie's death understood. I need to be more accepting of my doubting self, recognizing that I am a believer and a skeptic all wrapped up into one. As I learn to accept the whole of myself, embracing the conflicting aspects of my personality, both the believer and the skeptic, I will be true to myself.

But the underground guilt leftover from childhood intimidates me. It stifles my courage to embrace my deepest, truest self. The hidden guilt sabotages me and makes me hesitant to proclaim what I intuit from the depths of my being. It bullies me into asking questions looking for reassurance rather than making direct requests and bold statements about my beliefs. I had allowed doubt to undermine my faith in the belief that the mysterious and wonderful coincidence of the lights going out at the moment of Charlie's death was a miracle.

In spite of the encouraging dream and all the reassuring incidents, I still had a distance to go to reconcile the doubting and the faith-filled aspects of my personality, as my experience in Rome would reveal.

13

Faith

Am I dreaming?
Or is it you?
The "feather lady" asks
No dream
But truth
Whispering on the wind

A year and a half after Charlie's death, I still felt this interconnectedness between the two of us and that Charlie was very much a part of me. If I was beginning to doubt this connection between the two of us, the dream reconfirmed my belief on one level. But, in spite of the reassuring dream, after so much time alone, living one day after the other without Charlie's physical presence, the little seed of doubt was beginning to sprout inside me. So when I was planning a trip to Rome, I wrote in my journal, "Will you be with me, Charlie, when I am in Rome?" The doubting part of me didn't allow the believing part of me to write, "Be with me in Rome, Charlie."

It was now more than a year after the snow in the California desert and I was wondering if I would feel Charlie's presence again when I traveled. Certainly at home in my familiar environment, I knew Charlie was with me. The feathers in my path reminded me of his continued presence. I felt him in the garden and in our home. I felt him when I was talking on the phone with my daughters and when I was in the company of friends and family. But the seed of doubt was always present. "Is this all in my imagination?" My doubting self wondered.

In the back of my mind lurked an unsettling memory. On a flight to Boston, shortly after Charlie died, I sat next to a gentleman who planted a seed of doubt in my mind. The seed had lain dormant during the first year after Charlie's death when the experiences of his presence were so frequent and so intense. The man told me that his wife had died a little more than a year before. When I told him how I had experienced Charlie's presence, he told me that he, too, had had similar experiences of his wife's presence after she had died.

"After a while these experiences don't happen any more. They go away", he told me with certainty in his voice. I was annoyed with him. I didn't want to hear what he was telling me. I wanted to believe that the experience of Charlie's presence would be with me always. I resentfully pushed the man's comments away into the deep recesses of my mind.

Certainly, if what he said was true, I did not need to hear it so soon after Charlie died while the pain in my heart was so raw and while the awareness of his presence was so comforting. I needed the comfort of Charlie's presence in order to survive the pain of each day's emptiness without him.

Shortly after seeing Charlie in my dream, my friends, Annamarie and Sergio, invited me to visit them in their apartment in Rome. I was delighted to travel to Rome for Holy Week and Easter. It seemed a perfect time to visit Rome to celebrate the Jubilee Year with thousands of pilgrims from all over the world. Still unaccustomed to traveling without Charlie, I decided that I would go to Rome, not so much as a tourist, but as an observer.

I wasn't feeling very adventurous, so I thought I could manage if I went as an observer just allowing the treasures of Rome to unfold before me. I would not immerse myself in tourist guides before or during the trip, but allow the sights and sounds of the Eternal City to seek me out.

When Charlie and I had traveled together I had always been the one with my nose buried in tour guides reading about unique places and special treasures to visit. I once led the whole family through the streets of San Francisco's Chinatown until we found the restaurant that the guidebook said made the best pot stickers, a Chinese specialty we had never eaten. Pot stickers became a family favorite, a symbol of the determined, adventurous spirit that we shared and that bound us together. Our vacations became family treasure hunts. I lost this adventurous spirit when Charlie died. New places didn't hold the same fascination without my faithful traveling companion. The treasure hunt vacation no longer had appeal without someone to share the determined seeking and the excitement of locating the treasure. So I decided I would be content to just observe, to take my chances stumbling upon treasure rather than seeking it out.

Each day I wandered about the Eternal City by bus and on foot, enjoying the city's sights and smells, observing its inhabitants and the rituals of Roman life. I visited ancient ruins, modern buildings and the city's many churches. On Easter Sunday, Annamarie and Sergio and I went to St. Peter's Square along with thousands of other pilgrims from all around the world for Mass celebrated by the Pope. Tears came to my eyes as the three of us stood at the fringes of the huge crowd as the Holy Father gave his special Easter Blessing. I was missing Charlie.

Hoping that many of the tourists would have left after Easter, I planned to spend my last day in Rome at the Vatican, visiting the Basilica and the Vatican Museums. I arrived by bus early in the day and, failing to get off at the right stop, I found myself deposited at the Vatican Railroad Station. The station was deserted. The adjacent tourist center was empty but for a few employees. Feeling terribly alone, I stopped to have a cup of strong, black Italian coffee hoping to find in its caffeine the courage to go on. As I finished my coffee there was still not a soul in the station. I got up from the counter and forced myself to face the loneliness of the empty station. I proceeded down the long platform and then down a winding ramp that led to St. Peter's Square.

With each step I was painfully aware that I was alone, that Charlie, my traveling companion of 30 years was not with me. When I noticed a street person in shabby brown clothing coming up the ramp in the opposite direction, my fear and anxiety intensified. My pulse quickened as we exchanged sidelong glances. I hurried down the ramp. Only when the beginnings of the white marble colonnade that encircles the Square came into view did I allow myself to breathe a sigh of relief and slow my stride.

Now I was no longer alone, but I felt like a lost soul in the midst of the growing number of pilgrims milling about the huge square. To quiet my racing heart I focused on the usual tourist tasks. I wandered about the Square looking for the Vatican Post Office in order to mail post cards with special Vatican stamps. I found the post office, bought the stamps, licked them, placed them on the postcards, and deposited them into the mail slot.

Still overwhelmed by the anxiety and emptiness that hounded me, I crossed the Square again and went to the nearby souvenir shops to look for figures to complete a crèche I had bought years before. Comparing prices in different shops distracted me sufficiently from the painful loneliness that I felt, so that finally I was able to join the long line of Jubilee Year pilgrims waiting to enter the Basilica through the Holy Door.

Surrounded by groups of singing nuns, jubilant youth groups carrying colorful flags, and pilgrims from all over the world speaking languages I didn't understand, I relaxed enough to feel the embrace of the anonymous crowd about me. I spoke with no one, but I allowed myself to be swept along by the crowd's enthusiasm and goodwill. Once inside the Basilica I followed the throng, first viewing Michelangelo's eloquent Pieta behind its bulletproof enclosure and then stopping to admire the magnificent marble cherubs that adorn the holy water font at the entrance.

67

As I moved into the nave of the Massive shrine and meandered among the milling crowd, on two occasions I saw a monk dressed the way Charlie was in my St. Patrick's Day dream. Each time I attempted to move closer to the monk he disappeared into the crowd.

Charlie was very much on my mind as I approached the main altar. I gazed at the magnificent dome as I circled the great black marble pillars that support the canopy above the altar. Behind the main altar a Mass was being celebrated at another altar. I made my way to the back of the crowd around that altar just in time to take communion. In a few moments the Mass was over and I was about to leave to continue exploring the basilica, when I heard bells ringing. A procession of priests in flowing white vestments was making its way to the altar to begin another Mass. I found a seat in the pews as the priests began to concelebrate Mass. A nun played a small organ while the congregation sang unfamiliar hymns in Italian. High above the altar a stained glass window shed its golden light upon the scene below. The window intrigued me. I had seen a similar one in a little Orthodox Church in a square in the old part of Rome where my friends lived.

On Holy Thursday morning while walking through the cobblestone square on the way to the bus stop, I noticed people going into a dingy building. The building's dark façade had no sign announcing its purpose, but statues stood behind black iron grilles at both sides of the entrance. I was curious so I opened the wooden door. It led into a small, dark vestibule with two doors flanking each side of the tiny space. As I turned to the left and pushed the heavy wooden door open, the fragrance of incense and a bright golden light flooded my senses. A few dark, wooden pews were set at an acute angle on each side of the altar. About fifty people crowded the little church to capacity. Tall, colorful, gilt-edged panels decorated with images of Jesus and the saints with golden halos separated the pews from the altar. Three dark-bearded priests dressed in simple but elegant gold and red vestments led the congregation from the altar, which was partially obscured by the painted panels.

In the first pew, three young nuns in white habits with black veils covering their heads sang without accompaniment. Their melodious voices filled the little church with ethereal and haunting chants. The holy sound resonated in the sacred space as light from the stained glass window high above the altar intermingled with the incense-filled atmosphere. White-yellow light in the center of the window was radiating from the image of a dove with its wings spread wide. The Holy Spirit! The breath of God! I heard it in the nuns' voices; I saw it in the glow of suffused light; I smelled it in the fragrant incense. I felt its presence all through my body. I was immersed in the presence of God.

So when I noticed the dove in a similar design in the stained glass window at St. Peter's, I thought a picture of it would serve as a remembrance of my profound experience in the little Orthodox Church. I took out my camera to capture the scene: many priests in white concelebrating at the simple marble altar with the high altar with its golden angels and saints and bishops in flowing robes towering over it and the radiance of the dove shining on the scene from its oval window. I snapped the shot.

A moment passed. While I gazed at the altar the flame of one of the six candles on the altar went out. As a curl of smoke rose upward from the candle my body began to tremble. Powerful emotions flooded my body, surged through my soul, and emerged as salty tears.

Charlie had answered my question. A single candle extinguishing itself had sent a powerful message to me. Charlie is with me; I am not alone. With the extinguishing of the candle's flame, the doubt

69

I voiced in my question, "Will you be with me when I am in Rome?" was extinguished as well.

But knowing how the doubting part of me won't let itself be so easily snuffed out, with trembling hands I raised my camera and, through my tears, focused the lens on the altar with five lighted candles and one unlighted one in order to capture the scene on film. I would need visible proof in the future in order to renew my faith in what I knew without a doubt in this moment: Charlie is with me wherever I am.

When the Mass ended I was still sobbing. Picking up my belongings I wandered aimlessly amidst the throng of tourists in the great nave. When I spied another monk and attempted to follow him, he too melted into the bustling crowd. Then I descended the steps to the crypt of the basilica where St. Peter's remains lie. Wiping tears from my eyes, my body still shaking, I followed the flow of tourists as it meandered past the tombs of the popes, including the sarcophagi of more recent popes, Pius XII and John XXIII.

As I arrived at the exit and I emerged into the light of day, I controlled my trembling body sufficiently to ask the first Jubilee Year volunteer I saw how to get to the Vatican Museums. He startled me by answering, "Thank heavens, you speak English." He then explained that having spent hours answering questions in many different languages, he was relieved to be able to speak to me in his own tongue. At that moment, the floodgates holding back my emotions opened and I recounted the story of the candle. He listened as I told him of the lights going out at the moment of Charlie's death and of the significance of the candle extinguishing itself.

To my attempts to convey the awe I had experienced, he simply replied, "Things like that happen." He was puzzled when I asked if I could take his picture, but he agreed. I would need another photo for further confirmation when my disbelieving self would re-emerge and begin to doubt whether all these little miracles had actually happened.

My spirits buoyed by my experiences in Rome, I returned home filled with a sense of awe, reassured that Charlie is still with me wherever I am. I told my daughters, my friends, and my co-workers about my experiences at St. Peter's.

One Saturday, soon after I arrived home, friends invited me to a dinner party. BeeJee had set a beautiful table with a candle floating in water in a crystal glass at each place. When we were relaxing together after a delicious meal, they asked me to tell them of my trip to Rome. After telling them about all the famous sights I had enjoyed, I told them of the light of the candle going out at St. Peter's. A few moments passed and the conversation had moved on to another topic, when Richard interrupted the conversation and turned to me, saying, "Pauline, your candle has gone out." Tears of awe filled my eyes.

How fortunate I was to have another little miracle happen in the presence of friends, another little miracle reconfirming all the other miracles confirming that Charlie still lives. Could I have any doubt that Charlie is with me wherever I am? Could my doubt survive such an event witnessed by others?

I was growing stronger. Yet I would experience depression before I would discover that there was still something more I needed to do. In order to integrate these two aspects of my personality I still needed to learn not to suppress my doubt but rather to embrace it.

71

14

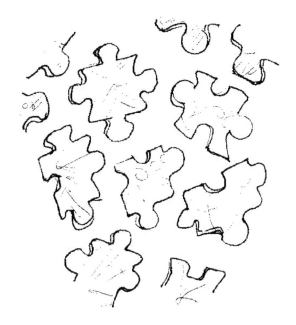

Confusion

Together on the outside
Hurting on the inside
I love the mornings
So why do I let myself lie in bed?
Like a funny smell
I sniff around and then ignore it
A sense of going crazy
Not wanting to take responsibility
I want decisions made for me.

More than a year passed. During that time I kept the story of the candle in my heart. Frequently, in the evening at home I lit a candle and enjoyed the comfort of its flame and fragrance. Each time a family member of a friend died I gave a candle to them to remember their loved one and as a reminder that their loved one still lived. My sister Kathy reported to me that one evening she lit the candle I had given her in memory of Charlie and was speaking to him in her mind. Just as she heard herself saying to him, "You're a good man, Charlie Flynn," the candle's flame went out. I treasured the story of her experience as another confirmation of Charlie's continued presence in our lives.

As the months wore on I settled into the single life, feeling more competent living alone, traveling all over the world with family and friends, creating a social life that was satisfying, and enjoying my career. But in the midst of what appeared to be a satisfying life, I began to experience a nagging feeling coming from deep inside me. I felt it was telling me that there was something new I needed to do. Although all the aspects of my life were satisfying, I sensed that there was something more that would give me an even greater sense of wholeness.

One by one I accomplished all the personal and professional goals I had set for myself after Charlie died. I learned to contra dance. I took singing lessons. I joined a yoga class and enrolled in an intensive year-long study of family therapy. I took my youngest niece and nephew, Dianne and John, on a cross-country vacation. I considered going back to school to study religious anthropology and I contemplated buying a place in the country.

Yet the nagging persisted. It wasn't superficial. I sensed it was coming from the deep recesses of my soul. Friends told me to be patient, saying, "With time you will know what it is you need to do." Yet I felt a sense of urgency and, as the year wore on, I worried that I was becoming depressed. Often I was sad and teary and didn't know why.

Charlie began appearing in my dreams more often but in disturbing ways. In one dream he was homeless and had a gray-green mold growing around his nose. I found the image unsettling and couldn't understand the message in the dream, so I wanted to dismiss it and forget about it. But I couldn't. I knew the dream had a message for me.

I found myself crying often. I didn't want to admit it, but I was depressed. Why? When I surveyed all the aspects of my life, I saw that I had a good life. It was a life that was both enjoyable and meaningful. I felt surrounded by supportive friends and family. I had a lovely home with a delightful garden that I cherished. I had a rewarding job as a pastoral counselor doing meaningful work helping people that I enjoyed. There seemed to be no reason why I should be depressed, but I surely was.

I tried to fight the tears by being optimistic, but some part of me would not respond to the positive outlook I was trying to put on. I continued to be teary often, at home, in church, reading a book, even looking at a picture of my grandparents on their wedding day. When I wasn't able to discern a pattern to my weeping, I became discouraged.

Finally I went back to see Molly who in the past had been a spiritual guide for me as well as psychotherapist. With her help I listened to my tears and discovered truths about myself that at some level I knew but was afraid to face. She helped me face the reality that I needed to write about how faith and doubt formed my journey through grief and to tell the story of *Charlie's Gift*. With Molly's help I found the courage to face the doubt I harbored, and to embrace the belief in the miraculous meaning

75

Pauline Dotzler Flynn

embedded in the events surrounding Charlie's death. I began to acknowledge both Charlie's doubt and my doubt as real and to recognize that the many incidents surrounding lights, candles, and feathers would not have happened without the doubting parts of our personalities.

Although I had journaled almost daily since Charlie was diagnosed, and since his death, putting all my thoughts and feelings into a coherent story would help me to discover the elements necessary to integrate these two warring aspects of my personality.

15

Paradox

Ambiguity is my name
Certainty feels so nice
Doubt can be as certain
Mystery - I'm all around

L istening to my tears led me down a path to a new understanding of faith and doubt. I began to see how my response to my parents' righteousness had caused me to lose myself. No wonder I was depressed. I had lost my center.

Righteousness is all around us. We see it in political affairs and in the religious world. It is the reason we say it is not a good idea to discuss religion or politics at social events. But righteousness also permeates our everyday lives too. I remember the couple I counseled who argued over the "right" way to put dirty dishes into the dishwasher. Righteousness certainly permeated my parents' relationship.

Being right, believing that one has the right way or the right answer, whether it is the right way to worship God, the right solution to the world's problems, or the right way to load the dishwasher leads to righteousness and separation. When we have such strong faith in our own ability to know the absolute truth, we cut off possibilities for real communication. This is where a little doubt can be helpful. It can bring us together rather than separate us. This is true whether we are loading the dishwasher or discussing our political beliefs or our religious faith. A little doubt goes a long way to helping us acknowledge the limits of our human understanding. By acknowledging ambiguity and uncertainty we become open to the vast complexities of life.

We humans have a tendency to shore up our faith with righteousness rather than to admit that we don't have all the answers. This tendency toward righteousness seems to be part of the human condition. It serves to make us feel strong and invulnerable. This is where the illusion lies. When our certainty, when our faith, isn't open to uncertainty or doubt, it binds us to rigidity and inflexibility and closes us off from any real communication with people who have a different point of view.

This happens in many relationships. This is what happened in my parents' relationship. When my father would disparage my mother's beliefs she held to her convictions with an even greater force. She left no room in her thinking for uncertainty. She dismissed his doubt and her own. In dismissing his lack of faith she closed herself off from listening to him, so that a dialogue between them never happened. They were stuck in polarized positions that cut off any possibility for communication.

Dialogue becomes possible when we hold to our faith but also acknowledge our uncertainties recognizing that there are other ways to view the world. **Faith and doubt are friends**. **When faith and doubt are friends, our faith can actually grow. This is the paradox.** Doubt is not the enemy of faith. Doubt is what allows us to be humble enough to listen to other perspectives even if they are different from our own. Suppressing doubt doesn't strengthen our faith. It rigidifies our faith and doesn't allow it to grow.

Since my parents were caught up in their own righteousness, my mother in her righteous faith and my father in his righteous lack of faith, I never wanted to allow myself to become righteous. I could see the detrimental effects it was having on our family. Living with their righteousness was painful to me as a child so I chose to question my own beliefs. If others didn't agree with me, I allowed their disbelief to undermine the strength of my own convictions. I began to look outside myself for verification. In this way I lost my center. I didn't understand that faith and doubt could be friends.

Once I knew what I needed to do, I experienced a greater lightheartedness, my tears began to subside and my depression began to lift. Writing the story of *Charlie's Gift* would help me to embrace my doubting self as well as my faith-filled self.

As I began to write this story and embrace the conflict within myself allowing faith and doubt to coexist, I had the satisfying sense that I was headed in the right direction. By embracing both parts of my personality, I would become true to myself.

But much confusion still lay ahead. My faith was yet to be tested as I learned to embrace my doubting self.

16

Ambiguity

Beyond the breakers
Dolphins frolic
A leaping duet
A trailing crowd
They say "come let's play"
Which one of them is you?

At Christmastime my oldest daughter Liz became engaged to her longtime friend, Philip. I was very happy for Liz because Philip is a strong and gentle person with solid values. I was pleased that they were ready to commit their lives to each other. However, after the joy surrounding the announcement of their engagement, I began worrying about how to manage all the practical issues related to the wedding without Charlie's help. Who would walk Liz down the aisle? Who would give her away? Who would help me make decisions about all the necessary arrangements?

I planned an engagement party for Liz and Philip for April 1, 2001, April Fool's Day. Charlie loved April Fool's Day as he never let an opportunity to have fun go by. Each year he found a way to make the day memorable. I wanted everyone at the engagement party to enjoy Charlie's sense of humor as a way of experiencing his presence. I decided that I would read to the guests a letter that Charlie had written to Liz when she was working in Harbin, China, some years before. I had written to her about her cousins who were getting married or having babies. She responded by sending a letter addressed to us that read:

> *Dear Abby:*
> *Everyone I know is getting married and having babies. What should I do?*
> *Lost in Harbin.*

So Charlie responded to Liz with this letter:

> *Dear L. H.*
> *Cheer up. It is very natural to feel sadness and sympathy toward friends and relatives who are less fortunate than you. Try to look at*

82

it objectively, and tell yourself they should have observed from the world around them that the dumbest two things they can do are 1. to get married and 2. to have babies.

The ones who get married should have known better because they grew up in families in which the senior members got married a long time ago, thinking "opposites attract" was just a cute, catchy saying. Then they learned it means one of them squeezes the toothpaste in the middle and the other would prefer to roll it up from the bottom. One wants to spend hours working in the garden and the other thinks it's perfectly okay if oak trees sprout from uncleaned gutters. One needs a bigger house to save old stuff and the other would rather get rid of the clutter and move to a modern condo.

The ones who have babies are even dumber. A baby uses about a million diapers. It takes 14 months (by actual count) before the baby understands as many words as the family dog. After you teach it to talk and to stop using diapers, you have to teach it to stop playing in mud and poison ivy. Then you teach it to drive and it moves away to another state. Then you teach it another language and it moves away to another country.

Some even have more than one baby. This just compounds the error. Each one uses another million diapers. Each one takes over a year to get smarter than the dog. They teach each other to play in mud and poison ivy. They get chicken pox in succession. Finally they all move away and your only consolation is your secret wish that some day they will be foolish enough to get married and have kids who are just as much trouble to their parents as they were.

You ask what should you do? I could advise you to try to warn your surviving friends and relatives of the hazards of getting married and having babies, but I know from experience that they won't take your advice. Leave the advice-giving to me.

   --Abby

The living room was full of friends and family listening attentively to me as I read the letter while holding back the tears that were forming in the corners of my eyes. Charlie's tongue-in-cheek humor evoked laughter in the crowd, just as it might have if he had been there. I felt good about that.

When I finished reading the letter, John, my friend Cora's husband, came to me to tell me that the dining room lights had gone out. Would I show him where the circuit breakers were so he could turn them back on? Thinking that someone had leaned against the dimmer switch and turned it off by accident, I tried to turn it on. No response. I tried again, still no response. I took John down to the laundry room and showed him the circuit breaker box. But the circuits were all on! We were puzzled. Why had the light gone out if the circuit was okay?

By the time John and I returned to the dining room, Cora and Claudia, my two very best friends, were laughing together. While John and I were gone they had realized that it was Charlie who had turned out the lights. When we pressed the light switch now the lights came on! I should have known–it was just like Charlie to take advantage of April Fool's Day to have a little fun and make sure that we were still aware of his presence in our lives.

Again my faith was encouraged but I would soon learn that my faith wasn't strong enough to live with the ambiguity that is an unavoidable part of life.

17

Impatience

My mind is cluttered with old stuff
In a million different languages
I'm foolish enough to think
I can put it all in English

Puzzling through the clutter
I try to find the light
All my eyes see is
Ambiguity

S hortly after his death I decided that I wanted to memorialize Charlie in some lasting and meaningful way. Because he was so passionate about his work in public service, I decided to establish a summer internship for a law student from his alma mater in the U.S. Attorney's Office for the District of Columbia, where Charlie had spent the major part of his career. I thought that by establishing this internship I could encourage law students to consider working in the field of public service, not a very lucrative area of law practice, but one that was so important to Charlie that he had dedicated his life to it.

Before funding the second summer's internship I wanted to talk with the first year's intern to discuss whether the internship had been helpful to him and to gather any suggestions he might have for improving the experience. We met for brunch on Good Friday at a downtown restaurant. While talking with the intern I became confident about my ability to structure this internship in a way that would honor Charlie's values and achieve the goals I envisioned. After our meeting I stopped in at a Good Friday service in one the nearby churches and then I took the Metro home. As I walked home from the Metro station I felt confident that what I was doing in establishing this internship was a good thing. I was proud of myself.

As I entered the house, feeling satisfied with myself and the efforts I was making to keep Charlie's legacy alive, I opened the front door. The first thing that I noticed was that the lights on the screened porch were on. The lights were Christmas twinkle lights that I had installed with Katie's help around all four sides of the porch at the top of the screening. A remote switch in the dining room controlled them.

When I stepped into the house and I saw the hundreds of little white lights twinkling all around the porch, I didn't feel comforted and reassured, as I had been when the lights went out when Charlie died, or when candles went out. Instead, the lights evoked a very unsettling feeling in me. I felt like I was being harassed. I was annoyed because I didn't understand what these events meant.

Questions nagged at me. What more do I need to do? Why don't these kinds of things happen to other people? What do they mean?

Shaken and unsettled by this experience, I turned to my best friend Cora for answers. "What do I need to do?" I asked her. She suggested that I talk to a priest whom we both admired because he was so down-to-earth and yet so very wise. He was someone we both felt could cut through all the confusion caused by these events and get to the heart of the matter. So I made an appointment to see Father Jim Connor in his office on the Georgetown University campus. Father Connor had given Charlie the last sacrament and said his funeral Mass. He had also come to the house to say Mass to help me and my daughters and my siblings and their spouses celebrate the six-month anniversary of Charlie's death as well as commemorate the 100th anniversary of my father's birth.

While Father Connor had helped me find a way through difficult moments surrounding Charlie's death, I came away from our meeting feeling like he hadn't really understood me. When he said to me, "It's time to let go of Charlie and move on", I felt he hadn't comprehended the events that kept recurring. I was trying to let go.

It was Charlie who was hanging on!

I wasn't turning these lights on. Charlie was.

I was trying to move on, do new things, and create a life for myself.

Pauline Dotzler Flynn

Charlie was hanging on…

Father Connor also suggested that I read the apparition stories, scripture stories about Christ appearing to the disciples after his death and resurrection. Since the meeting hadn't given me the calming answers I was looking for, I decided to wander about the campus, enjoying the fragrant flowering trees and beautiful plantings, hoping to find a sense of peace and relaxation. I headed toward Dahlgren Chapel to pray before I left for home. I sat awhile on a bench in the courtyard garden outside the chapel, concentrating on the colorful tulips, the dramatic reds and yellows and vibrant purples, trying to calm myself.

I entered the dimly lit chapel. Its dark wooden pews and vaulted ceiling enclosed a dusky space. After a few moments a priest began to light the candles on the altar and I realized a Mass would soon be starting. I decided to stay for the service. During his sermon, the priest discussed the apparition stories! Just moments before Father Connor had suggested that I read those stories and now I was hearing a sermon on those very stories! What an amazing coincidence! Only this time, the coincidence didn't comfort me. It merely compounded my unsettled feelings. In my agitated state the only part of the sermon that I heard was the priest's conclusion that the stories tell us that "Jesus is within reach, but not within grasp."

Then I remembered that, just a week before at the Easter Vigil service, our pastor Father Byron had begun his sermon with the question, "What is the practical meaning of these events?" And that question became a mantra for me. What is the *practical* meaning of these events? I needed to find the answer to that question.

88

18

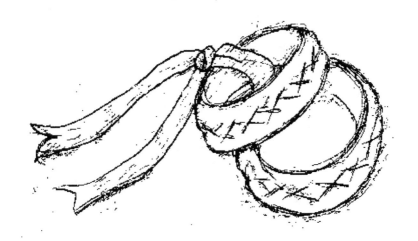

Intertwined

United in love
We go our
Separate ways
For a while

W hen I arrived home from Georgetown there was a message on my voice mail from the local library. A book I had reserved was being held for me. I hadn't remembered what book I had reserved, but I went straight to the library to pick it up. Waiting for me was *"Love is Stronger than Death–The Mystical Union of Two Souls"* by Cynthia Bourgeault. I thought to myself perhaps this book would offer an answer to my question.

Back at home I settled onto the screened porch for the evening, reading the New Testament stories of the apparitions as Father Connor had suggested and the library book. It was a balmy evening and I sat alone under the bright overhead light enjoying the soft spring breezes while I read the biblical stories over and over. I read Bourgeault's little book from cover to cover. Finishing the book, I laid it aside, disappointed because it had concentrated on the philosophical and theological aspects of a relationship with the dead, not on the practical aspects of one's relationship with the deceased.

I felt discouraged. I needed an answer to the questions. What is the *practical* meaning of these events? What did all these experiences that I was having mean? What should I do about them? So, disappointed with the book and having read the apparition stories over and over again without getting any new insight, I let go of all the compulsive searching for answers.

Emotionally exhausted, I leaned back into my chair and said to myself, "Our lives are intertwined." As I heard myself say the word "intertwined," my attention, which was so inwardly focused, was jarred out of its reverie by a soft click, and hundreds of little white twinkling Christmas lights came on. Lights which Katie had hung around the porch for the holidays were now all aglow! It was as if the proverbial light had come on. Only it had actually happened. The light bulb in my mind went on simultaneously and I finally understood. Here was the answer I had been searching for–**Charlie and I–our lives are intertwined!** I had known this from the very beginning, but now I understood it on some new and deeper level.

(As I write these words the telephone's ring interrupts me. When I answer someone asks for Charles Flynn and I say, "I am sorry, he is deceased." Usually when a telemarketer asks for Charles Flynn I say, "He is not here." I don't want to get the caller upset. This time I say, "He is deceased." because I don't need to protect myself any more. I know that being deceased does not mean that he is not here. Then I think jokingly to myself Charlie will live forever with the telemarketing industry.)

This was not a new discovery that our lives were still intertwined even after Charlie's death. A part of me had known from early in our marriage that our lives were intertwined. I had written that word many, many times in the journaling that I did in the early days and weeks and months after Charlie died. I had even decided to have our wedding rings melted down and made into one ring for me. The matching design on our wedding bands was of two strands intertwined and I had hoped to find a jeweler who would melt down the gold from the two bands and recreate a similar design on a hammered background. What I hadn't realized is that this design is called a love knot, having two strands intertwined with no beginning and no end. But in my early journaling and even in the plans for melting down the rings I had not consciously understood what I was aware of on a subconscious level. I was becoming more consciously aware that Charlie and I were still intertwined.

Yet I still did not understand what the *practical* meaning of this intertwining was. Did it mean that I shouldn't let go, that I needn't move on? If Charlie is within reach but not within grasp, what did that mean? I still had a way to go to understand the practical meaning of these events.

19

Inevitability

A wave is born
It swells
Arcs
Then tumbles and crashes
To a watery grave
In a sea of foam
In its demise
It recedes
Into another wave.

I couldn't continue writing Charlie's story. I was too confused, too unsettled by the events to be able to put my thoughts into any coherent form. So I journaled frequently, merely recording events and the feelings they evoked in me.

Attempting to make practical meaning of the events nagged at me. That's the kind of person I am. I remember someone saying about me, "Pauline's always thinking." It's true. I like to have things make sense and my mind gravitates to discovering meaning. Now it was working overtime in an attempt to make meaning of all these events. Learning to live with ambiguity continued to challenge me. I was still trying to make sense of my experience rather than to merely embrace it.

I would need more time to allow faith and doubt to coexist in me.

Loneliness

At dawn's first light
 I can see the spray
The dolphins make
When in their play
They break the surface
Not seen later in the day
Are you there when I don't see you?
Do you fill the
Empty spaces between things
When I am not looking?

ecause Liz and Philip's wedding date was drawing near, I had to put these anxious feelings aside in order to concentrate on planning the details of the wedding. Since the wedding was to be on the East Coast while they lived on the West Coast, I agreed to look for a site for the wedding and to select a caterer. In order to find a beautiful outdoor location for the wedding and the reception I spent one whole day driving alone through the nearby Virginia countryside. This was an excursion I would have taken with Charlie had he been alive. I missed his company and his thoughts about each of the possible locations for the wedding, but I enjoyed the new spring green of the rolling hillsides and the brashness of the dashing creeks. I felt peaceful. I was alone but I didn't feel lonely.

Somewhere along the way I lost my reading glasses that day. I usually wore these glasses on a chain around my neck. These were the same glasses that Charlie had reached for on one of the last days before he died. As he tugged at the glasses hanging from the chain around my neck, I thought he was trying to tell me that he wanted his glasses. When I handed him his own glasses he frowned and pushed them away. He continued to yank at mine till I took them off and handed them to him. He clumsily tried to put them on himself.

I was puzzled by his action and I couldn't make sense of it at the time. He wasn't able to speak and I was unable to help him make himself understood. So the meaning of his action was hidden to me. But I kept the memory in my heart. Now the glasses were gone.

The wedding date was September 22. There were many decisions to make and I missed Charlie's opinions. I was excited when I found, Fresh Start, a non-profit organization that employed formerly homeless people and trained them in food preparation and service. Fresh Start's profits went to training people who had formerly relied on soup kitchens for their sustenance when they were homeless and unemployed. Since Charlie had wholeheartedly supported SOME–So Others Might Eat, an organization that feeds the homeless, I knew that he would have concurred with my decision. Fresh Start went a step further than SOME. It addressed the underlying issues behind unemployment and homelessness by teaching marketable skills to those who were unable to support themselves.

The wedding date was fast approaching when the country was devastated by the terrorist attacks on the World Trade Center and the Pentagon. I was alone that morning relaxing on the porch when Liz called from California to break the terrifying news. Never had I felt so alone. One airplane was still in the air and no one knew what would happen next. Living just a few miles from the Pentagon, the Capitol and the White House, I felt vulnerable. Feeling alone as I did in Rome didn't compare with feeling alone during this national crisis. Without Charlie here to turn to for advice and comfort in a time of extreme danger I found being alone so intimidating that I invited myself to my neighbors' homes so I would have companionship as the day's events unfolded.

I was scared, but all my fears for myself were put aside by a phone call from Laura. Her roommate Maile had gone to New York for a conference at the World Trade Center and hadn't been heard from. I tried to allay Laura's worst fear by telling her that conferences were usually held on the ground floors of hotels and that would have made it easy for Maile to escape. "Mom," she replied, "The conference was on the 106th floor." The buildings had already collapsed. It seemed there was no hope. Laura and her other roommates, including Maile's sister, Marilese, and their college friends, telephoned rescue agencies, and searched the internet for news of Maile and survivors. Day and night they searched looking for some sign of hope that she might have survived, even making trips to New York and visiting hospitals.

Upon awakening on the morning of September 12th I went to my computer to continue my usual journaling. There, on the seat of the yellow chair we call Charlie's chair, were two feathers, one solid gray and one gray with touches of gold. Both feathers had floated down from the wreath of feathers hanging on the wall above the chair. Seeing them lying there next to each other, quill to quill, I knew with certainty that Maile was gone, that she had died in the terrible inferno and collapse. I knew that she was with Charlie, and that she was safe.

With the feathers lying on his chair, Charlie was telling me that Maile was with him and that she was at peace. This was such horrible news to think that this beautiful, thoughtful, and gentle young woman with so much potential had perished. Yet, I felt strangely comforted knowing that she was safe.

As the days wore on with the recognition that no one who attended the conference had been heard from, my awareness was verified. Eventually Maile's remains were found and delivered to her parents in Hawaii. Maile loved the oceans. She had spent her junior year of college at Mystic Seaport studying and sailing the oceans. When her ashes were strewn into the Pacific by the flotilla of family and friends on surfboards who had gathered to honor her, a sea turtle rose from the deep to greet them. The turtle's presence comforted them.

The world as we knew it was gone forever. But life goes on, even in the midst of all the pain and suffering and the contradictions we are attempting to reconcile.

21

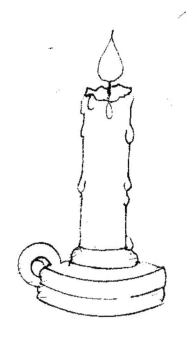

Timelessness

Time alone
Time together
What is this time now?
Togetherness?
Aloneness?
All mixed up in one

Pauline Dotzler Flynn

The wedding day arrived, a comfortably warm autumn day. The bride was radiant in her white silk dress with its lace bodice and softly flowing skirt; the groom was confident, strong and tall. Together they greeted their guests. In the walled garden while Liz and Philip exchanged vows the songs of birds drifted down from the canopy of tall trees that shaded the historic garden. The birds, messengers of the spirit and mediators between heaven and earth, were announcing that Charlie was present as were all of our loved ones who had gone before us. We celebrated the love of Liz and Philip and the love of all those present, all the friends and family who surrounded them in this love-pledging ceremony.

At dusk, when the sun was setting behind distant trees and the light of hundreds of votive candles on the tables was shimmering in the twilight, I stood to the side surveying the scene. I knew in that moment that it was the enduring nature of love that protects us and binds us together. I knew that all of our loved ones were present. They were present not just in the photo displays which Philip's mother, Ardy, and I had created of our parents' and grandparents' wedding days. Charlie and his parents and grandparents and my parents and grandparents as well as all of Philip's grandparents were there with us. They are the angels who surround us with love.

In that graced moment I experienced the power of love to cross all dimensions of time and of space. I knew without a doubt that the transcendence of love enables us to live beyond the grave.

There is no dying, not if there is love. Love crosses all boundaries. It cannot be confined. Time and space cannot limit love. Love has no limitations.

100

Those who have gone before us love us as if they were here with us. They watch over us. They are closer to us than we know.

All of our lives are intertwined. Indeed, the bonds of love are stronger than death.

Pauline Dotzler Flynn

22

Miracle

Angels abide
But still I cry
Tears of sadness
As well as tears of joy
My soul made tender
Sorrow becomes
Gratefulness

Yet I am still left with that ultimate question. What is the *practical* meaning of these events? How do I live my life with this understanding of the power of love across time and space?

I pray differently now. I open my heart. I pray love. I pray love to all the people in my life–my family, my friends, my clients. I pray love to world leaders, those whom I support and those whom I oppose. I pray love to my friends and family who are ill and I believe that they can experience this healing love I send no matter where they are, right here in town or in California where my friend Joan is battling metastatic ovarian cancer.

I am more aware of my heart as the source of love. I feel my heart beating when I pray and I feel the pulse of the beating hearts of those I am sending love to. All the attributes that flow from love–peace, kindness, gentleness and patience, as well as wisdom, courage, and strength of will are ours if we open ourselves to love. If we let the love in, all these attributes are ours. Allowing ourselves to know how much we are loved, we can love freely.

When I look at my life objectively, I do not see that the way I live my life is radically different from what it used to be before I had this awareness. Fear and anxiety still invade my psyche, but not as powerfully, not as frequently. My faith is stronger, my doubting side is less dominating. I am able to take on the doubt and put it aside. Yet, I can embrace the skeptic in me. I am learning to tolerate ambiguity and the anxiety it brings. In learning to live with not knowing, with not understanding, I can open myself up to mystery. I am more open to being myself and embracing life just as I experience it. Love is the source of my courage to face life's continuing challenges.

There is one important new understanding. When it had come to me, I don't know. I understand now, that on that day when Charlie reached for the reading glasses that hung around my neck and attempted to put them on, he was answering my question, "Will you tell me when the angels come for you?"

What seemed like the confusing actions of a dying man was really a profound statement of an enormous reality. By reaching for my glasses and attempting to put them on himself, Charlie wanted me to know that **THE ANGELS WERE THERE IN OUR MIDST** and that they had come for him. He could see them and he wanted me to be aware of their presence. He was telling me I have only to look and I will see!

When his actions confused me and I didn't understand what he was trying to tell me, he didn't stop trying to get my attention. So he put the lights out as he left this life. When I still didn't appreciate the presence of angels in the peacefulness we experienced as we sat with him in the candlelight as he was leaving his body, he played with candles and lights and strewed feathers in my path. Just like Charlie to persist in his playful ways until I got the message and understood what he was trying to tell me!

I see now that the miracle we needed and which I asked people to pray for was happening even as Charlie lay dying.

And the miracle continues.

Pauline Dotzler Flynn

23

Well-being

In the pulsing beat
Of my heart
I feel
Universal love

In March of 2002 I was having symptoms that caused my doctor to recommend a bone marrow biopsy. While I was optimistic that the breast cancer that I had had 15 years before was behind me, I had the biopsy. But during the biopsy, in overhearing the little quiet whisperings between the nurse who was assisting and the doctor, I knew that the results of the biopsy would not be good. Returning home from work on the day I was expecting the doctor to call with the results of the biopsy, the phone was ringing as I opened the front door.

As I dashed up the stairs to get the call I noticed that the little Christmas twinkle lights on the porch were lighted. I knew! I knew that it was the doctor calling with the biopsy report and that the report would indicate that there was a new cancer. But the lights, the lights they encouraged me!

I picked up the phone. I knew that Charlie was with me. I knew that I would be okay. I was afraid, but I knew that I would be held within the power of Charlie's love and God's love and the love of my friends and family. I knew that I was embraced in love and that love would protect me and strengthen me, maybe even heal me.

My faith, at long last, was stronger than my doubt.

This was Charlie's most important gift to me.

I have faced down my doubt in a way that allowed me to go to on a pilgrimage to Lourdes and pray for a miracle for myself. I asked God to heal me with the living water that flows from the spring at the Grotto.

That's not to say that there isn't a little bit of doubt. That's me. Now I can say with a chuckle, "I know that's okay." The miracle continues.

24

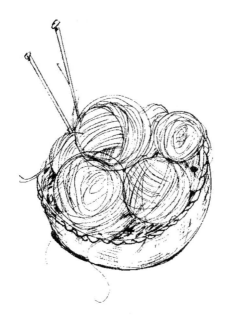

Transformation

The Muses

The muses come quietly
Make a stir
Then quickly steal away
Even more quietly

Pauline Dotzler Flynn

Electric Chemistry

Electric chemistry, no silly toy
But a precious gift
A love knot
With no beginning and no end

Wired into you
Our fates intertwined
I was going crazy
Trying to live without you

I was haphazard
Numb
Till we made a new connection
Transforming me

In candlelight's soft glow
The veil of eternity fades
Revealing a new vision
In its own time

110

On Sleeplessness

Is there a purpose to this sleeplessness?
Thoughts swirling through my head
So random
In perpetual motion
I am grouchy inside myself
Finding fault with people in my mind

The ablutions of the day are a blessing
Putting one foot in front of the other
Am I numb or really in pain?
Is it just a matter of time?

What I do remember is the life we lived together
Always a sacred place where we could just talk
We were good for each other
Two heads better than one
Confronting the days together
The challenges, the joy
The irritations, the invitations

Missing the framework you gave my life
I clear out the old unspoken dreams
And take with me
Your tenderness in my heart
Your constancy in my bones
Your wit and wisdom in my mind

These are hard days, hopeless days
These are silent days, days of realism
Yet days of wisdom and hope
Oh, that seems like blasphemy
No wonder sleepless nights

Pauline Dotzler Flynn

I Get Discouraged

I get discouraged
Feel uninspired
Life's too vague
The muses don't come

Your presence is palpable
Your spirit permeates me
My being giving you a place in this world
While you reside in another

Is this the devil taking control of my soul?
Some one told me so
No, there is meaning here and I am awakened to it
My life will never be the same

On the path to enlightenment
I am protected by love's generosity
Flowing back and forth between the generations
Taking me beyond yesterday's discouragement

Without our salty tears
The oceans would empty
The glories of sunrise and sunset
Fill our eyes with hope

A Feather in My Path

Alone I fear
In my pain
And in my sorrow
But the deep
Abiding connection we share
Is more profound
Than when distracted by life's exigencies
You know me
My pain, my fear
My love, my joy
I am not alone
You walk with me
A feather in my path

Pauline Dotzler Flynn

A Star on My Shoulder

A star on my shoulder
A feather in my path
A wave in the ocean
A song in the air
A bird on the wing
A breeze in the morning
The light of a firefly in the gloaming
In the dark of the night
A voice
A presence

Tenderness

Time is on our side
Every day you are
Near me
Dear one, over here, over there
Ever present
Reserved in your own quiet way
Never too loud
Each time of connection
Significant
SIGNIFICANT

In Sacred Space Inside Me

I am not afraid of my sense of inadequacy
Trying to describe the day
And what is happening inside me

The instruments come together
As if hired by someone else
Wanting to create a sacred space
In vacant dreams of mine

My passion lies beyond the tears
A bit of jealousy beneath the awe
There are surprises here
I never imagined

In sacred space
Inside me
I reach to the heavens
And bring it down to earth

Pauline Dotzler Flynn

Faith is My Middle Name

I asked my tears, "Who are you?"
They answered,
"You are not ready to hear my name.
You wouldn't understand.
You are mired down with stuff
You don't do anything about.
I am hard to get.
Reaching for the spirit, elusive
You need to clear a space
To go beyond."

"Open up to possibility
That Poetry is good for you.
Who you are at the core of your heart
Is what you like to do,
A blessing in disguise."

Listening to my tears
As they washed over me
At the depth of my being
I saw the beauty of the universe
Closer to my vision.

And to my tears I cried,
"You teach me who I am.
I am an ecumenical person
In a more compatible place.
I am missing something
Unless I can express it in real time.
Faith is my middle name."

116

I Love the Mornings

I love the mornings
So why do I let myself lie in bed?
Together on the outside
But hurting on the inside
Like a funny smell
I sniff around and ignore it
I want decisions made for me

Has anyone ever counted the leaves of a tree?
But summer doesn't last forever
This new life feels like stumpy branches
And winter's blank whiteness
I do not know where I am going
I want decisions made for me

Learning from experience like Frederick the mouse
I've stored up memories on summer morns
And now that winter is here, hop out of bed
And greet the day, life's new season
With the warmth of summer on my face
And the smile of leaf green in my heart
This is where I need to be

My Mind, My Heart

My mind questions
Remains confused
My heart embraces
And is satisfied

117

Pauline Dotzler Flynn

'Til Dragonflies Hover

As children play
A dragonfly hovers
Its gossamer wings
Overshadowing life's miseries

As the sun sets
Your light permeates the atmosphere
With a pink and purple glow
That surrounds me

Day is done
The night is nigh
I could be lonely
I could be sad
But for the breeze
A silken veil that
Caresses my arms

Oh gentle breeze
Embrace my heart and my soul
Let me fly with you
Till the sun rises
And children play
And dragonflies hover

118

Head and Heart

My head wants to understand
Your presence
Still with me
Telling me that everything is OK
Every day
Right now
Yearning to know

My heart knows
You are here beside me
Still
Telling me not to worry
Every day
Right now
Yearning heart, knowing heart

My head wants to know
How it can be
That you are here with me
Right now
Every day
Telling me not to worry
I'll be ok
And is confused

My heart yearns to understand
How it can be
That you are here
With me
Right now
Every day
Telling me not to know
And is satisfied

119

Pauline Dotzler Flynn

Paradox

Paradox
    Is a woman
    No one has ever met

No one has yet to find where she lives
    Yet everyone knows her
    And has come upon her some time in their lives

Some people imagine
    She is young and beautiful
    With smooth skin and silky hair

Others believe
    She is an old woman
    With craggy bones and a wrinkled face

Sometimes she is friendly
    And warm
    And inviting

At other times
    She can frighten you
    With her demanding presence

She goes by other names
    Mystery and Craziness
    Foolishness and Wisdom

Her real name is LIFE

A Wave

You are a wave
    in the ocean that
        catches me
            by surprise

I dive into you and
    you are gone

Once again
    With each passing wave
        I feel love

Pauline Dotzler Flynn

Rosemary

Your Own Sweet Self

Grasp a sprig of rosemary
Hold it close
Breathe deeply
Let the flames of fragrance
Light the inner spirit
With the glory and radiance
Of your own sweet self

What Does Closure Mean?

Set on the shores of life alone
You are like a distant dream
Confused, I do not know what I need to do
Nor when or where to take the next step
I do not know what closure means

Muddling through the day, the night
the weeks, the months
the years
I feel sick to my stomach
I do not know what closure means

Fear blocks my vision, my energy
Fear of losing control
Fear of fear
I am afraid to be passionate
I do not know what closure means

Nor what makes grace happen
Yet I step into the unknown
With more faith in myself
And my right to be in the world

I walk across the fears
Flatten them out
But the fear lingers
Yet the mind quiets

The spirit takes reign
Opening up to mystery
My life is an offering in a new way
This is what closure means

Pauline Dotzler Flynn

This poem, written by Leigh Hunt (1784-1859), was one I memorized as a child. Its lines have stayed with me through the years. It seemed especially poignant after Charlie's death. Years later, when I recited the poem at my brother Jim's funeral service, I discovered that both my sister, Kathy, and my brother, Robert, knew the poem by heart as well.

Abou Ben Adhem

Abou Ben Adhem (may his tribe increase!)
Awoke one night from a deep dream of peace,
And saw within the moonlight in his room,
Making it rich like a lily in bloom,
An angel writing in a book of gold:
Exceeding peace had made Ben Adhem bold,
And to the presence in the room he said,
"What writest thou?"—The vision raised its head,
And, with a look made of all sweet accord,
Answered, "The names of those who love the Lord."
"And is mine one?" said Abou. "Nay, not so,"
Replied the angel.—Abou spoke more low,
But cheerily still; and said, "I pray thee, then,
Write me as one that loves his fellow-men."
The angel wrote, and vanished. The next night
It came again, with a great wakening light,
And showed the names whom love of God had blessed,
—And, lo! Ben Adhem's name led all the rest.

--Leigh Hunt

The following poem, My Grandfather's Clock, was put to music in 1876 by Henry Clay Work. The lyrics of the song were from an original poem by C. Russell Christian who wrote the poem about his grandfather, James P. Christian.

My Grandfather's Clock

My grandfather's clock was too large for the shelf,
So it stood ninety years on the floor;
It was taller by half than the old man himself,
Though it weighed not a pennyweight more.
It was bought on the morn of the day that he was born,
And was always his treasure and pride;

125

Pauline Dotzler Flynn

But it stopp'd short… never to go again when the old man died.
Ninety years without slumbering, tick, tock, tick, tock
His life seconds numbering, tick, tock, tick, tock
But it stopp'd short… never to go again when the old man died.

In watching its pendulum swing to and fro,
Many years he had spent while a boy;
And in childhood and manhood the clock seemed to know,
And to share both his grief and his joy.
For it struck twenty-four when he entered the door,
With a blooming and beautiful bride.

But it stopp'd short… never to go again when the old man died.

My grandfather said, that of those he could hire,
Not a servant so faithful he found;
For it wasted no time, and had but one desire,
At the close of each week to be wound.
And it kept in its place, not a frown upon its face,
And its hands never hung by its side.

But it stopp'd short… never to go again when the old man died.

It rang an alarm in the dead of the night,
An alarm that for years had been dumb;
And we know that his spirit was pluming for flight,
That his hour of departure had come.
Still the clock kept the time,
With a soft muffled chime,
As we silently stood by his side.

But it stopp'd short… never to go again when the old man died.

126

Author's Request

Dear Reader,

I believe that the experiences I had after Charlie's death are not unique. Many people experience meaningful coincidences, little miracles, or communications after the death of a loved one. Because our scientific and technological culture does not acknowledge and support experiences that are out of the ordinary or spiritual in nature, there is a tendency to dismiss these experiences as mere coincidences or figments of the imaginative mind.

If you have had similar experiences after the death of a loved one, I would like to hear from you. Please write to me at the email address below:

Pauline.flynn1@ymail.com

Praise for *Charlie's Gift*

" . . .an unflinching look at the mystery of love, how we struggle to understand inexplicable events and how we can learn to tolerate uncertainty and ambiguity. Pauline Flynn traces the challenging path of widowhood, all the new tasks that must be learned, and shares the heartache of loss, doubt, and loneliness. She emerges from the dark, her path lighted, and her heart as light as a feather–intertwined forever with the love of her life and blessed by her Christian faith.

~ Georgia Robertson, Ph.D., Grief Counselor and Poetry Therapist in Washington, D.C.

Pauline Flynn's book is a wonderful look at how we can grow in our grief. Anyone who has dealt with the loss of a loved one will find this book provides hope and promise, even in the dark days. *"Charlie's Gift"* is a gift to every bereaved individual. Here we see the journey of one woman, who, guided by the love and connection to her husband, finds the strength to go on with a meaningful life. This book will help others on their journey. Pauline helps us recognize that truly, "The bonds of love are stronger than death."

~ Dana G. Cable, Ph.D., Professor of Psychology and Thanatology, Hood College.

Pauline Flynn's sensitive chronicle of her husband's life, death, and continued legacy provides a rich and honest account of her grief journey. *Charlie's Gift* is a resource I will recommend to grieving widows and widowers who grapple with the normal, but painful healing process that leads them in search of meaning and solace following their tremendous losses.

~ Robin McMahon, Ph.D., Clinical Social Worker and Grief Therapist, former Director of the Grief and Loss Program at Hospice of Northern Virginia.